CONTE MAGGI'S
MILLE MIGLIA

Also by Peter Miller

The Fast Ones
Men at the Wheel
From Start to Finish
Aces Wild
The Billion Dollar Oil Fraud

CONTE MAGGI'S MILLE MIGLIA

Peter Miller

ST. MARTIN'S PRESS · NEW YORK

First published in the United States of America in 1988
All rights reserved. For information, write:
Scholarly and Reference Division
St. Martin's Press, Inc., 175 Fifth Avenue, New York, NY 10010

ISBN 0-312-02525-4

Library of Congress Cataloguing-in-Publication Date applied for

Typesetting and origination by
Alan Sutton Publishing Limited
Printed in Great Britain by
WBC Print Limited

For
Angela, Nicholas and Sophia
with love

CONTENTS

FOREWORD

I have pleasure in writing these few lines with my best wishes for the book, which tells the story of Aymo Maggi's life as a sportsman. Aymo and I rarely met every day, but we were frequently together during the many occasions of the Mille Miglia, in which I first raced in 1930. I had a deep admiration for Aymo, who always showed his real devotion to the sport of motor racing in such a sincere and decisive way.

PIERO TARUFFI
Rome, November 1987

In the 1952 Mille Miglia, Piero Taruffi was used as pace-maker for the Ferrari team. He is seen here after leaving the Vicenza control in the 4100 cc Ferrari Vignale, having made up 6 minutes on Cotton's Delahaye No. 608 (*Publifoto*)

Competitor in fifteen Mille Miglias and winner of the last race in 1957, died January 1988

Conte Aymo Maggi, founder of the Mille Miglia

PREFACE

Few will deny that during its thirty year existence between 1927 and 1957, the Mille Miglia earned the reputation of being the best road race in the world.

It was spectacle, it was circus and it was a tough, unyielding challenge over 1,000 miles through the Italian countryside. The Mille Miglia produced thrilling victories and humiliating defeats but, most of all, it created champions. To win at Brescia was to have reached the pinnacle of sporting achievement.

Although each of the original 'four musketeers' — conte Aymo Maggi, conte Franco Mazzotti, Renzo Castagneto and Giovanni Canestrini — played their individual part in the Mille Miglia, it is Maggi's biography that I have written. It was he, an Italian nobleman whose family history could be traced back more than seven centuries and who became a racing driver of repute in the 1920s, who cajoled and fought to sustain the race and never lost faith in it.

When any famous incident in history — a thrilling triumph such as the first trans-Atlantic flight or a tragic loss such as the sinking of the *Titanic* — is analysed, a combination of circumstances will always be found which made that event possible. If any one factor had been

HRH The Prince Michael of Kent, left, before the running of the 1987 Mille Miglia for historic cars, with Contessa Camilla Maggi and Bruno Boni, President of the Brescian Chamber of Commerce (*Foto Eden, Brescia*)

CONTE MAGGI'S MILLE MIGLIA

altered then the event could not have happened. So it was with the Mille Miglia.

The pride of the people of Brescia had been shaken when after their first running of the Italian grand prix in 1921 the event was taken from them in 1922. The Italian automobile industry was in decline and motor sport generally in the doldrums. The Italian people needed a champion, and when Maggi in 1925 and 1926 suddenly started winning major motor races, though only with a foreign car, they found one. Interest in motor sport was rekindled, the Mille Miglia was born and its critics silenced after the first race

in 1927 when the first three places were taken with OM, Officine Meccaniche, cars built in Brescia. In the eleven post-war events after Italy had been shattered by war, conte Maggi's Mille Miglia became the focus of national interest until its tragic end in 1957.

The Mille Miglia was unique. It could never be copied today; public opinion would not tolerate the thought of drivers motoring at speeds of 200 mph on open roads through towns and villages. But from 1927–57 the Mille Miglia was a part of the lives of millions, and it is in conte Aymo Maggi's memory that I have

written this portrayal of a man who dreamed an impossible dream and saw it come true.

It was never my intention for this book to be a comprehensive race by race account, or a technical description of the cars which took part. But I hope that in these words and dramatic photographs we will remember those racing pioneers of the Mille Miglia and thank them for their courage.

Peter Miller
1988

ACKNOWLEDGEMENTS

My thanks to contessa Camilla Maggi for allowing me to write this biography. I hope it will bring her pleasure and recall happy memories of Aymo Maggi, the man who made the Mille Miglia into the finest motor race in the world.

Thanks also to those two worthy champions of the Mille Miglia, the late Piero Taruffi and Stirling Moss, for their contributions and the joy they have given race fans all over the world with their skill and courage. And to Aymo Berardi, Guido Berlucchi, Bruno Boni, Alessio Brunelli, conte Carlo di Castelbarco, Peter Davidson, Neil Eason-Gibson, Giacomo Ragnoli, Manuel Vigliani and others for historical background material and research.

And thanks too, to Enzo Ferrari – *pilote, che gente*, Giannino Marzotto – *La Ferrari alla Mille Miglia*, Alberto Redaelli – *Le Leggendarie Mille Miglia* and conte Giovanni Lurani – *la Storia della Mille Miglia*, for the help of their books for reference and permission to use extracts, and particularly to 'Johnny' Lurani for permission to reproduce the route maps prepared by the Istituto Geografico De Agostini, Novara, 1979.

In preparing this book, I have researched material going back to the turn of the century. While every effort has been made to credit individual photographers – or, at least, those who provided the pictures – in some cases the sources have been too obscure and the origin untraceable. To these donors, too, I give my thanks.

1 | THE FOUR MUSKETEERS

'No driver could ever say that he had achieved his victor's laurels if he had not won at Brescia.'

ENZO FERRARI

The Mille Miglia was born in the third-floor apartment of the celebrated Italian motoring journalist, Giovanni Canestrini, in via Bonaventura Calvieri, Milan on the evening of 2 December 1926. On Sunday, 12 May 1957 it died, banned for ever by the Italian government.

For thirty years the Mille Miglia had been run on the open roads of Italy, a mix of spectacle and sport that had created its own legends, and considered by Stirling Moss and many other drivers to be 'the finest road race of them all'. But before beginning to understand the race, or what it stood for, and looking into the background of the 'Four Musketeers' who conceived the legendary event – conte Aymo Maggi, conte Franco Mazzotti, Renzo Castagneto and Canestrini himself – listen to the words of commendatore Enzo Ferrari. Ferrari, now ninety, who was present at every one of the twenty-four Mille Miglias, as a driver, team director and constructor – 'No driver could ever say that he had achieved his victor's laurels if he had not won at Brescia.'

Conte Aymo Maggi, who will always be remembered as the father of the Mille Miglia, was born in Brescia on 3 July 1903. By Italian definition he was simply a nobleman, a person of extreme wealth

The 'four musketeers', founders of the Mille Miglia: left to right, Conte Aymo Maggi, Conte Franco Mazzotti, Giovanni Canestrini and Renzo Castegneto (*Alfa Romeo*)

CONTE MAGGI'S MILLE MIGLIA

Casa Maggi, the family home at Calino, near Brescia, which has belonged to the Maggi family since the sixteenth century

Conte Aymo Maggi, aged nineteen, in one of his first races, in 1922

people of Brescia to cheer about and they needed something new to excite them. Brescia had had a long tradition since before the turn of the century as a centre for motor-cycle and automobile racing and was also a pioneer in the field of aviation. On 4 September 1921 the first Italian grand prix had been held on the Fascia d'Oro circuit at Montichiari, Brescia and Maggi, then nineteen, had seen the Frenchman Jules Goux win in his Ballot at nearly 90 mph. From that moment he knew nothing would prevent him from becoming a professional driver.

This win by a French car and driver in the inaugural grand prix caused an outrage in the Italian national press and there was fierce criticism of their faltering automobile industry. There was also a strong lobby by the automobile club in Milan to go ahead with the building of the new race circuit at Monza, outside the city. The lobby was led by Arturo Mercanti, a wealthy entrepreneur, who though considered a man of honour was a *bresciano* only by adoption. Through his efforts construction on the autodrome progressed rapidly and in 1922 the Italian grand prix was 'stolen' from Brescia and switched to Monza. Even when Mercanti was killed during action with the Italian army in Abyssinia in 1936 and awarded the gold medal for Military Valour, the citizens of Brescia, proud of their long heritage of motoring tradition, never forgave him for robbing their rich industrial city of its country's grand prix.

So it was in the winter of 1926, while returning to Brescia from a hillclimb event at nearby Nave-San Eusebio, that Maggi dreamed of instituting a motor race for sports cars unlike any that Italy had ever seen. Immediately he arrived in Brescia he telephoned his old friend Castagneto and booked a table for dinner at the famous Vecchio Cova restaurant in Milan

and privilege, someone perhaps who did not need a mission in life, a gentleman-farmer who could have continued to grow the lively Franciacorta wines for which the region had been famous for centuries. Yet when he died in 1961 at the age of fifty-eight Maggi had

achieved an impossible dream. He had created the finest motor race in the world – and that shall be his epitaph.

At the birth of the Mille Miglia in 1926, Maggi was already one of the best known racing drivers in Europe, but apart from his successes, there was little for the

Conte Aymo Maggi, aged twenty-three, before the start of the first Mille Miglia held on 26–27 March 1927. Maggi chose to drive the most formidable car of the seventy-seven starters from Brescia, a 7370 cc 8-cylinder Isotta Fraschini, with Bindo Maserati, one of the four Maserati brothers. After eleven refuelling stops and three tyre changes they returned to Brescia in 22 hours 35 seconds to finish sixth, an average of 46.2 mph

CONTE MAGGI'S MILLE MIGLIA

for the evening of 2 December, where they met conte Franco Mazzotti and Flaminio Monti, a wealthy motoring enthusiast from Brescia.

Mazzotti, nick-named Kino, was born on 31 December 1904 and was seventeen months younger than Maggi. The boys had grown up together, becoming lifelong friends and sharing an intense love of motor-cycles, cars and any type of competition involving speed. Mazzotti learned to drive on the family estate at an early age and used to race one of his father's saloon cars on his own slalom events around the marble columns surrounding the courtyard. Self-controlled, thoughtful and creative, he became an enthusiastic and experienced pilot. Having learned to fly in his early twenties, he later took part in numerous long-distance races and completed an adventurous trans-Atlantic crossing in 1934. He encouraged Maggi to learn to fly and was delighted when his friend obtained his wings, but disappointed that he never really shared his passion for flying. Later, Mazzotti became equally absorbed by motor racing and he drove successfully in many events. He also sponsored a team of Bugattis for the first Italian amateur racing team, the 'Scuderia per dilettanti'.

When Renzo Castagneto had met Maggi in the mid-1920s, he already had a reputation as a superb organiser of sporting events with an eye for the smallest detail, and a flair for press and public relations. Castagneto was born in Padua in 1892 and went to live in Milan as a child. As a young man he was a skilled racing cyclist, and later scored many victories on motor-cycles. In the early 1920s he was a successful journalist and in 1923 became director of the weekly sporting newspaper Lo Sport Bresciano. Castagneto then moved into

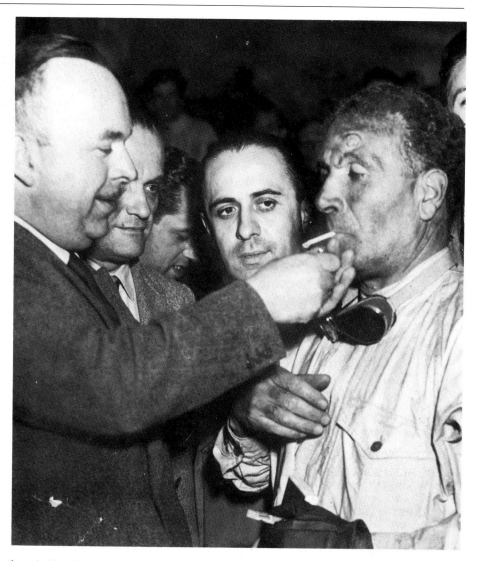

A superb picture showing the strain of driving and winning – the Mille Miglia. Seen here (right) in 1948 after winning his third Mille Miglia victory is Clemente Biondetti. He won again in 1949 and his four wins in 1938, 1947, 1948 and 1949 were never equalled. Born near Sassari in 1898, Biondetti was a successful motor-cycle racer until forced to retire after a serious accident; he became a travelling salesman, and even bought and sold bananas to pay for his racing car. His victory in the 1938 Mille Miglia changed his life and after his last race, he said: 'How can you not wish Brescia well? It is Brescia which gave me life and confidence again.' (Neil Eason-Gibson)

the organisation of major sporting promotions such as the Gira d'Italia cycle race — Italy's equivalent of the Tour de France — and the motor racing grands prix of Bari, Messina, Syracuse and Tripoli. He was also a football fanatic and was secretary of the Brescia Football Association for many years.

After dinner at the Vecchio Cova, Maggi, Mazzotti, Monti and Castegneto drove round to Canestrini's apartment in the via Bonaventura Cavalieri, where Maggi shouted up to him that they had important business to discuss. While Monti excused himself for not staying, Maggi, Mazzotti and Castagneto went upstairs and hammered on Canestrini's door.

Giovanni Canestrini, the fourth 'musketeer', was born at Rovereto, south of Trento in 1894 and moved to Milan with his family as a youngster. On leaving school, he started an engineering course at Turin Polytechnic, but this was interrupted by the outbreak of World War I. After serving with a mountain artillery battery until 1918, he volunteered as a pilot and was sent to the Venaria Reale air training school, where his chief instructor was Arturo Ferrarin who was to become one of Italy's most famous pilots. Canestrini served for forty months and became a much-decorated and experienced airman, with a keen interest in both aircraft and automobiles. On his demobilisation in spring 1924, Emilio Colombo, director of *Gazzetta dello Sport* in Milan, made him its motoring correspondent, a position he held for the next fifty years.

Canestrini let Maggi, Mazzotti and Castagneto into his apartment and there then followed an historic meeting as the 'four musketeers' argued late into the night. Maggi led the discussion in his typical dynamic style. 'There are no Italian cars available and if we want to

Augusto Turati, left, secretary of the Fascist Party and Mussolini's deputy, with Conte Aymo Maggi, second left, at the Coppa Acerbo. It was Turati who gave final approval to the first Mille Miglia in 1927

be competitive then we are forced to buy a foreign one. We cannot find any new type of event and it seems as though nobody is interested in motor sport any more. All our old traditions are slipping away and we must do something about it.'

A heated discussion started. It was obvious that a circuit race would be pointless, since Brescia had lost the Italian grand prix to Arturo Mercanti's Monza syndicate four years previously. It would have to be a road race — a tough test for drivers and cars that would also capture the imagination of the public. A Tour of Italy and an Alpine Cup race had both been rejected when Castagneto and Canestrini picked up a touring map

of Italy, looking for inspiration. 'What about Brescia to Rome?' one suggested, for at that time it was fashionable practice to race from city to city.

'No,' the other replied, 'if we did that, we would get only half the publicity, and Rome would get all the rest. Why don't we do Brescia-Rome-Brescia in one single stage?'

Mazzotti suddenly sat up, 'That sounds fantastic,' he said, 'and you won't have to worry about money. I will finance it. How far would it be?'

Castagneto, using his vast experience of marathon road events, replied, 'Sixteen hundred kilometres, more or less,' and Mazzotti, who as a pilot and navigator was accustomed to measuring in miles,

T o me the Mille Miglia was certainly the finest road race of them all, but although I loved it, I was always afraid of taking part.

Afraid because I was never really able to learn the route, and afraid because of the extremely high speeds we were getting. In 1955, when I won in the Mercedes with Denis 'Jenks' Jenkinson, we were travelling up to 180 mph on open roads. Although the brakes were very good and we had done sixteen training laps – which was a lot more than most of the drivers taking part – there was a constant, nagging fear that if anything went wrong there was nothing we could have done about it.

The crowds just stood in the road until the very last moment and then jumped clear, and Fon de Portago's fatal accident in 1957, when a left front tyre blew at speed, could have happened to any of us. Quite frankly, I am amazed that the race went on for the number of years it did, because every year the press and the government seemed to be increasingly worried about the fantastic speeds we could get when the roads were dry.

It was almost as though the organisers prayed for bad weather to dampen the roads down, as in 1956, when Eugenio Castellotti's Ferrari took one and a half hours longer in the torrential rain than I had done the year before. That way more media attention was focused on Eugenio's heroic drive against the elements, rather than his average speed, although that was still around 87 mph.

In the 1953 Mille Miglia Stirling Moss drove a C-type Jaguar with low ground-clearance. Special dispensation allowed him to start from the road beside the wooden starting ramp. This rare shot shows him looking up to the starter on the ramp above him, waiting for the off (*Neil Eason-Gibson*) INSET Stirling Moss after his superb 1955 Mille Miglia victory – his winning time of 10 hours 7 minutes 48 seconds was never equalled (*Neil Eason-Gibson*)

STIRLING MOSS

Stirling Moss, at the wheel, with navigator Denis Jenkinson, on their way to a record-breaking victory in their silver Mercedes 300 SLR in 1955 (*Mercedes*)

One of the things I remember most about the Mille Miglia was the wonderful hospitality of Aymo Maggi and the contessa Camilla at Calino. It was not in any way to do with Aymo's background of centuries of tradition, or with eating and drinking in pretentious style. It was just that we all thought that being at Casa Maggi during the race period was like being at home. The atmosphere was so relaxed and friendly and I always had the firm feeling that if I stayed at Calino before the race I would be lucky on the day itself. Maybe it was a superstition – but then I always was very superstitious.

In 1955 Neubauer at first insisted I stayed with the team at the Hotel Vittoria in the main square in Brescia, which immediately overlooked the scrutineering bays, but I said I wanted to be with the Maggis at Calino. He agreed after a while, but wrote giving his strict instructions about my training programme: I had to eat alone at 8 p.m., be in bed by 8.45 p.m., and get up at 5 a.m., so that my metabolism got used to the special routine of my start-time of 7.22 a.m. I will not say that it was strictly adhered to, as on the Friday before the race the Maggis gave their traditional eve-of-race party for hundreds of guests and Neubauer spotted that I stayed up for that. But generally the atmosphere at Calino was really wonderful.

When one of the Mercedes mechanics came out to collect me in a saloon car at 5.30 a.m. on Sunday morning of 2 May, I felt fine, although as always a little nervous and worried before the start. It was normally quite chilly around Brescia at that time of day, but it was difficult to know what to wear as it grew hot later on in the open car. So I wore my lightweight white overalls with the 'SM' initials embroidered inside my lucky heather emblem and a rally jacket, which I later discarded. We had a fabulous drive and it was nice to make a bit of Mille Miglia history together, as my time of 10 hours 7 minutes 48 seconds at an average speed of 98.53 mph for the 1,000 miles was never beaten.

CONTE MAGGI'S MILLE MIGLIA

The first Mille Miglia in 1927: Conte Aymo Maggi, in the Isotta Fraschini, before the start

exclaimed excitedly, 'That's one thousand miles. Why don't we call it a race for the *Coppa della Mille Miglia?* After all, the Roman legions used to calculate their marches in miles, why not follow their tradition?' With a shout, all four accepted the idea and the Mille Miglia was born.

Maggi, then only twenty-three, proposed that the new race should be entirely Brescia's responsibility and that their own automobile club of Brescia should be formed, rather than rely on the Italian Automobile Club of Milan. Although still not twenty-two, Mazzotti readily accepted the responsibility of presidency. Castagneto, the oldest of the four at thirty-four, became its first secretary and later its permanent director-general: he was to be responsible for the overall planning and administration of every one of the twenty-four Mille Miglias.

Canestrini promised to get his newspaper, the *Gazzetta dello Sport*, to promote the race, and it was he who first announced it to the world in the newspaper's pink edition under the

The first Mille Miglia in 1927: Conte Aymo Maggi, in the Isotta Fraschini, on the Raticosa pass, cheered on by Enzo Ferrari, far left

CONTE MAGGI'S MILLE MIGLIA

Conte Aymo Maggi at the start of the 1928 Mille Miglia in the 8-cylinder Maserati he drove with Ernesto Maserati

banner headline, 'THE MILLE MIGLIA CUP TO BE HELD DURING THE WEEKEND OF 26–27 MARCH 1927 WILL BE THE MOST IMPORTANT MANIFESTATION OF ITALIAN MOTOR SPORT EVER'. It was a prophetic statement, but the immediate reaction to Canestrini's news story was an avalanche of protest and criticism, mainly on the grounds that it would be impossible to administrate a race of such magnitude.

The response of the Italian Automobile Club was also negative and it was only through the foresight of its president, Silvio Crespi, who wrote a letter to Arturo Turati, the secretary-general of the Fascist party and second only to Mussolini himself, that an impasse was avoided. Turati had been born in and grown up in Brescia and was a personal friend of Maggi. It was therefore decided that Maggi should deliver the letter himself to Turati in his office in Rome. After a cordial meeting with Turati, who was too much of a sportsman not to realise how important such a prestigious race could be, Maggi emerged with a letter giving the official seal of approval not only for the Mille Miglia to be held, but also for the liaison between the police, the army and the civic authorities to begin immediately. That meeting between

Turati and Maggi was the 'moment of truth' for the Mille Miglia for it is certain that without their friendship the race would never have been run.

When Maggi drove back to Brescia with Castagneto, after the meeting with Mazzotti and Canestrini, he was a happy man and Castagneto recalled later that everything had changed for the better in those few hours. But neither of them could possibly have known what an unbreakable link they had forged. For if conte Maggi was captain of the good ship *Mille Miglia*, then Castagneto will always be remembered as his faithful and unflinching first officer. Already good friends in 1926 when the race was first conceived, Maggi and Castagneto epitomized the true spirit of the Mille Miglia, working together for thirty years through twenty-four editions of the race.

Castagneto was a superb organiser with an innate sense of showmanship and public relations and the ability to attract headlines for the race in the world's press. It was he who invented the traditional red arrow symbol, emblazoned with the words '1000 MIGLIA', which became known internationally and was the very essence of the Mille Miglia. It was to be seen everywhere: on flags, banners, lanterns, posters, bookmatches, ashtrays, scarves and in shops, bars and restaurants all over Italy. But, most important of all, the sign was adopted by Mille Miglia fans — the *tifosi* — who painted it in large red letters across entire roads from pavement to pavement, or from top to bottom down the side of a house on the Mille Miglia route, pointing the way for competitors to follow. Beneath the arrow, in equally bold letters, was painted the name of the local hero — NUVOLARI — TARUFFI — ASCARI — and alongside the words VIVA VIVA to speed him on his way.

Because of this the Mille Miglia became more than just an exciting sporting event; it was a sequence of spectacular incidents. The whole atmosphere in race week was electric, from the scrutineering of the cars in the piazza della Vittoria, to the night departure in the viale Rebuffone, when cars were flagged away from the wooden starting ramp by Castagneto.

By overcoming remarkable financial, political and technical difficulties Castagneto and Maggi were able to improve the event with each succeeding year. Through peace and war, through fog, rain and scorching heat, they plotted, schemed and argued to make the Mille Miglia the most prestigious road race in the world. But one thing that they could never have predicted was the Hall of Fame of drivers who would win the Mille Miglia over those dusty Italian roads in the next thirty years: Minoia, Campari, Nuvolari, Caracciola, Borzacchini, Varzi, Brivio, Pintacuda, Biondetti, von Hanstein, Marzotto, Villoresi, Bracco, Ascari, Moss, Castellotti and Taruffi.

2 THE MAN WHO LOVED LIFE

'For Maggi the Mille Miglia represented a way of life and the ideal which determined his every action.'

RENZO CASTAGNETO

From the moment conte Aymo Maggi was born in the family palazzo at via Musei, Brescia, northern Italy on 30 July 1903, it was accepted that as son and heir of a dynasty which could be traced back to the beginning of the thirteenth century, he would enjoy privileges that others would never know. But, throughout his life, although always aware of his aristocratic background and fiercely proud of his lineage, he was never arrogant, or abusive of his influence and power.

The Maggi family had been noblemen for more than seven hundred years. An early descendant, Emanuele Maggi, became mayor of Brescia in 1243; another relative, Berardo Maggi, was bishop, or *vescovo*, and Prince of Brescia from 1274 to 1308 and is still remembered by the street in Brescia bearing his name, the via Vescovo Berardo Maggi. In 1441 Sebastiano Maggi became vicar-general for the whole province of Lombardy; he was beatified by Pope Clemente XIII in 1760. The palazzo Maggi was rebuilt in 1540 by Onofrio Maggi and in 1677 a later Onofrio received the title of conte Maggi di Gradella by concession of Carlos II, King of Spain.

His father, Berardo Tommaso

Conte Aymo Maggi, c.1906, second left, with his mother, Anna, father, Berardo, and younger brother, Camillo

Francesco, born on 22 April 1866, married Anna Vignati, who was five years younger than him, on 24 September 1902. Maggi was the elder of two brothers – Camillo, who was born in 1904, sadly died of consumption at the age of just eighteen – and was brought up in an atmosphere of wealth and calm. His father, Berardo, a dedicated horseman, taught him to ride and shoot at an early age. When only ten-and-a-half months old he was lifted onto a horse's back to get the feel of the animal, and before he was three, he was

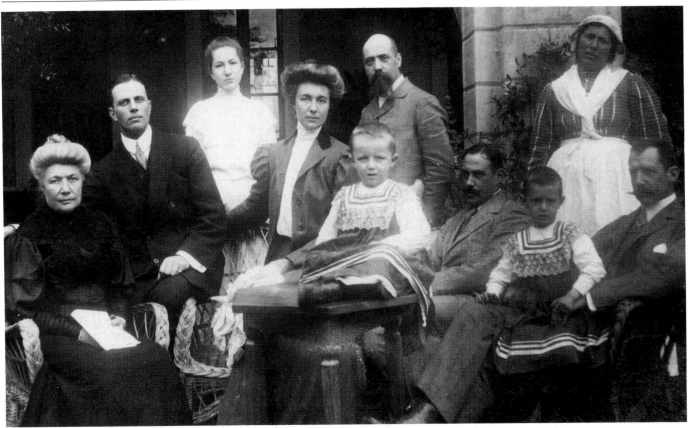

A family group at Calino: conte Aymo Maggi sits on his father's lap on the right, his brother Camillo on the table

Gradella, 1932

Conte Aymo Maggi's parents: conte and contessa Berardo and Anna Maggi di Gradella

Conte Aymo Maggi stands on the right of the family group in front of a touring car at Calo, c.1915

CONTE MAGGI'S MILLE MIGLIA

Conte Aymo Maggi aged ten and a half months, is placed on horseback by his father, Berardo

Conte Aymo Maggi, right, with his younger brother Camillo

On the beach at Pegli with his younger brother, Camillo, left

Conte Aymo Maggi jumps the pet donkey over obstacles laid out in the grounds at Calino

jumping his pet donkey over obstacles set out in the grounds. The estates were filled with horses and four-in-hand carriages, which Maggi's father drove all over Europe, but Maggi was more interested in the latest automobiles — driven by Maggi's father or relatives and wealthy friends — which could often be seen in the courtyards of Gradella and Calino. Brescia was already a pioneer of the newly-emerging motor industry and these were becoming increasingly popular with the Italian aristocracy in the years before World War I. It was this close association with the automotive world and its leaders which shaped Maggi's destiny. He learned to drive sitting beside the family chauffeur and soon became fascinated with the automobile, and speed of any sort.

Tall and restless, with a ready smile and ruthless determination, Maggi was very friendly with conte Franco Mazzotti Biancinelli, the son of a wealthy banker from Milan, who had a summer estate at Chiari, and both resolved to become racing drivers. By the age of twelve in 1915, they were obsessed with speed and competition. Often borrowing tools to lighten the frame and forks of their bicycles for their frenetic races round the grounds, the two boys were constant companions and they became skilled mechanics and engineers through working on joint projects, in which speed

On the yacht in the harbour with family and crew

Aymo and Camillo with their mother (centre, in white hat), surrounded by villagers at Gradella

Family tennis party at Calino

and more speed was paramount. Their competitive spirits were further fired by frequent visits together to the famous *Settimana Automobilistica Bresciana*, the Brescia Speed Weeks, where motor-cycles and cars were raced by the aces of the day and aeroplanes, airships and balloons were regularly displayed and often flown competitively from inside the race circuit.

It was also Mazzotti who later encouraged Maggi to take his private pilot's licence. But although Maggi gained his wings, he did not really enjoy flying or share the enthusiasm of his friend, already a highly-experienced pilot of international fame, and if there was any way of reaching a venue by car he would always drive. Maggi was never happier than when behind the wheel of a powerful touring car, luggage piled in

The Maggi family at an early Brescia air show, *c.*1912, TOP; and contessa Anna Maggi at the controls of a flimsy aircraft of the XIth Squadron

Early days of hot air balloons in Brescia: conte Berardo Maggi with family and friends

CONTE MAGGI'S MILLE MIGLIA

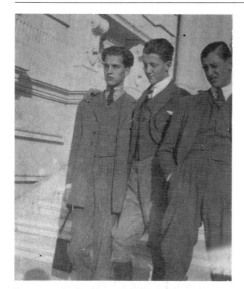

Conte Aymo Maggi, right, with conte Franco Mazzotti, centre, and Camillo, at the Villa Mazzotti in 1920

Conte Franco Mazzotti was a lifelong friend of conte Aymo Maggi. An experienced pilot, he is seen here flying his own aircraft in 1935. He disappeared without trace in a wartime flight over the Mediterranean

the back and driving in the toughest possible conditions.

As a young nobleman brought up on large country estates — the family spent a few weeks at Gradella in the spring, and the rest of the year at Calino — Maggi was well versed in the arts of hunting and shooting, taught either by his father or the servants. He was already an excellent shot as a boy, and later in life hunting was his favourite hobby away from the circuits. He was often invited to shoots both on nearby estates and elsewhere in Italy, but he was happiest when duck-shooting on his friend's property beside the marshes of the Venice lagoon. To Maggi, however, hunting was never a senseless slaughter; it represented a personal challenge, a test of his hands and eyes against the erratic pattern of fast-moving birds. He was a keen conservationist at heart and would never

Conte Aymo Maggi, third left, with a group of mechanics and drivers at the 1925 Rome grand prix, which he won. Conte Franco Mazzotti is on his right

Conte Aymo Maggi with a large group of relatives and friends at Gradella

An elegant Bugatti saloon at Gradella

Conte Aymo Maggi, left, and his brother Camillo in fancy dress c. 1912

Touring in the Dolomites with his father in 1919. This shot was taken in the Passo Tomale and Monticelli; conte Aymo Maggi is second left

The Maggi family in pony and traps in the courtyard at Calino

Conte Aymo Maggi attended an officer cadet's Military Academy in Rome and is seen here, left, with other cadets; BELOW, Maggi with his class at the Academy

hunt deer or game in the forest, and one of the family's favourite pets was a large wild boar, so domesticated that when called it would come out of the woods to take tea on the terrace.

At the end of World War I the family was deeply upset by the death of consumption of Maggi's step-sister, Nina; she was engaged to be married and only twenty-one. They went to live in an hotel in Rome for a year to get over their loss and there Maggi attended a military training school as a cadet, but on his return to Brescia went back to the local school. Although surrounded by horses, Maggi did not share his father's enthusiasm for them. He was still a very competent rider, however, and one day won a bet from friends for breaking-in a particularly fiery black stallion, which did its best to throw him across the cobbled yard.

In his spare time Maggi had started cycle-racing on Brescia's old dirt-track, where he was known as a tough and determined competitor, who neither gave nor expected quarter. He switched to motor-cycle racing in 1921 before completing his year's compulsory military service in a cavalry regiment, and in 1922 took up motor racing. He drove a Chiribiri and then turned to Bugatti, gaining numerous successes in subsequent years with Alfa Romeo, Bugatti, Maserati and OM, which was built at the Officine Meccaniche works in Brescia.

On 23 April 1931 conte Aymo Maggi married Camilla Martinoni Caleppio, whose father had been one of the early Brescian motoring pioneers in the early years of the century. The wedding was attended only by relatives and close friends, including both conte Franco Mazzotti and Arturo Ferrarin, the legendary Italian pilot of the Rome to

Conte Aymo Maggi was brought up surrounded by horses on the estates at Gradella and Calino. He is seen here with carriage and four, grooms and postillion

Conte Aymo Maggi and contessa Camilla on board the yacht *Raquettit* which they sailed in Mediterranean waters with friends

Conte Aymo Maggi with his father in the courtyard at Calino

Aymo, Camillo, family and friends on the lake at Gradella, near Milan

Tokyo record flight and Schneider Cup fame.

The Maggis honeymooned leisurely, touring the Italian and French rivieras, and returned to live at Gradella and Calino. Maggi's mother had died in 1928 and his father in 1929, when Maggi, aged twenty-five, inherited the large estates at Gradella and Calino and the title of conte Maggi di Gradella.

Both Aymo and Camilla loved to travel and they made many trips throughout Europe and north Africa, where they often visited Camilla's aunt who lived in Alexandria. While there they went swimming and sailing and visited the pyramids and tombs of ancient Egypt. For several years they kept a small ocean-going yacht in harbour at Rapallo, on the Italian riviera, which they used as a base for many happy sailing and fishing trips with friends. Maggi was an excellent water-skier and he and Camilla enjoyed swimming and diving from the boat on their Mediterranean holidays.

The Corinth Canal

The family at Gradella. Conte Aymo Maggi stands on the roof of the car at right

Superb action in this shot of conte Aymo Maggi (Bugatti) at the Sorrento–San Agata hill climb. Note the closeness of the crowd to the road. INSET LEFT An early hill climb event for conte Aymo Maggi, aged twenty-one, in 1924, driving his Fiat 501 at Garnano–Tignale. INSET RIGHT In the 1920s conte Aymo Maggi, as a leading Italian driver, was used in an advertisement for Cioccolota Lurati

Egypt: Camel racing at Luxor; in front of the pyramid and sphinx; Abu Simbel; Beggars' children buried in the sand to demand 'cadeaux' from tourists

Conte Aymo Maggi loved hunting and was an excellent shot. He is seen, TOP, travelling in style at a private shoot and, CENTRE, participating in a winter rough shoot after the war

This wild boar was extremely tame and frequently joined the family for tea on the terrace, before returning to the woods

When they were living at Calino the hospitality of Aymo and Camilla Maggi was almost as memorable as the Mille Miglia itself. During race week, the magnificent house became an extension of the race's headquarters in Brescia — the centre, it seemed, for the world's automotive industry, the constructors, the drivers, the team managers, the sponsors and most of the international press corps. On the Friday preceeding each Mille Miglia, the doors of Casa Maggi were thrown open for an unforgettable party, when senior government officials, the chief of police and leading civic dignitaries mingled with the entire Mille Miglia circus. The oak-beamed ceilings with their ornate panels rang with laughter and the sounds of conversations in many languages as the drivers tried to forget the thousand miles which lay ahead, while the Maggis welcomed their guests with natural charm.

At other times of the year there were dances, house parties, shoots and tennis tournaments and frequent meetings of the Automobile Club and the many committees on which Maggi served. He had a dynamic, gregarious and outgoing personality and some of his guests might have been excused for anticipating their visits to the family mansion with trepidation. But Maggi had a natural warmth and the ability to make his guests, whatever their background, feel completely at ease, so that within minutes of their arrival everyone would be relaxed and talking animatedly.

42

My friendship with conte Aymo Maggi goes back to the year 1925, when we first raced against each other on the Targa Florio in Sicily. From then on, we met regularly at circuits all over Europe and I was always impressed with his driving skill and mechanical knowledge. His cars were immaculately prepared and either Aymo, or his faithful mechanic Rino Berardi invariably made last-minute adjustments to the car so that it performed just that little bit better. I will always remember the day in 1930 when I arrived in Brescia for the first time in my position as the racing director of Mercedes-Benz, and we made our first tentative entry into conte Maggi's fantastic Mille Miglia with a single car. It was a powerful 7-litre Mercedes SSK model for the German pair, Rudi Caracciola and Christian Werner. It was really a test run for the following year but we certainly learned a lot, for although Rudi finished sixth overall, he was more than an hour behind Tazio Nuvolari's winning Alfa Romeo with his mechanic Gianbattista Guidotti.

Conte Aymo Maggi, beside the car door, and Renzo Castagneto, wearing his traditional bowler hat, at the start of the 1952 race with Juan Manuel Fangio's superb Alfa Romeo with bodywork by Touring, Milan

We came back the following year, with a lighter, more powerful Mercedes SSKL, or Super Sport Kurz Leicht, for Caracciola, accompanied this time by Sebastian, who scored a brilliant win by eleven minutes from the Giuseppi Campari/Attilio Marinoni Alfa Romeo and the Brescia-built OM of Giuseppi Morandi/Archimede Rosa, knocking eight minutes off Nuvolari's time of the previous year.

When one talks about the Mille Miglia, one naturally thinks first of its ebullient creator, Aymo Maggi, for after all he was its keystone: it wasn't just that he was such a talented driver, he was also an experienced official at the top echelon of motor sports' administration.

It was Maggi's detailed knowledge of the complicated regulations covering

international motor sporting events that really saved the day for us in 1952 at the official scrutineering of the Mercedes team in piazza della Vittoria in Brescia. We had entered three prototype 6-cylinder 300 SLs in the over 2000 cc sports class for Rudi Caracciola, Herman Lang and Karl Kling and these were fitted with the controversial 'gull-wing' doors. They were called this

ALFRED NEUBAUER

because the doors swung out and up to allow easy access and when fully open came to rest with the bottom level of the door over-hanging the road; with both doors open, and looking from the front of the car it really did seem like a sea-gull landing on water.

On our arrival at the square, which was thronged with people, we were handed a form, written in technical Italian, that we had never seen before and told by the scrutineers that the doors did not comply with international regulations. It seemed most likely that we would have to leave Brescia without being able to start – which would not have pleased my directors in Stuttgart at all. Then Maggi came bustling up, wearing his familiar dark brown hat with its slightly upturned brim, the habitual cigarette between his lips. With him was the celebrated French journalist, Charles Faroux, the race director Renzo Castagneto and a whole party of technical experts, ready to give their verdict on our claim that the doors were perfectly legal. In hushed silence, Maggi bent down with great deliberation and carefully measured the doors for height and width. Writing the figures slowly on the back of an envelope, he rose and said to the waiting group, 'Gentlemen, these doors do not contravene the regulations. There is nothing written to say whether doors should open horizontally or vertically so the Mercedes are completely within the rules. They may start in the race.' Thanks to his wisdom of King Solomon we were able to finish second and fourth overall to the Bracco/Rolfo Ferrari, although we did not win the race. But it is pleasing to see that directly as a result of Aymo's wise counselling that day in Brescia, this type of door-opening has since been used effectively in several competition cars.

It is not only the practical things that one remembers about this race of giants. It is the wonderful hospitality in the great château at Calino, which has been the home of the Maggi family for centuries. There, while the drivers

Conte Aymo Maggi, right, at the Mercedes team garage with, left to right, Alfred Neubauer (team director), Rudi Caraccioloa (half-hidden) and Charles Faroux with the controversial gull's wing car in 1952

and their co-drivers did battle, wives or girlfriends could relax for a little and enjoy its charm and that of the gracious contessa Camilla, whom I know had a soft spot in her heart for Stirling Moss, who was a frequent guest.

Now Maggi is dead and his last race is over. For us in the business of racing it has not been possible to live our lives in peace, for in order to achieve our passion for speed we have had to race every day of our lives. But as we survivors get older, we have one thing left to think about, and that is the paradise of the Mille Miglia, which Aymo allowed us to share with him. And whatever happens, that is something nobody can ever take away.

Giovanni Bracco, centre right, and Alfonso Rolfo, centre left, receive the impressive Coppa Trossi after their outright win in 1952 from conte Aymo Maggi, left, and Renzo Castagneto

The Rome grand prix, 1925. INSET LEFT, Conte Aymo Maggi works on his Bugatti during practice. The atrocious muddy conditions and narrow tyres did nothing to stop him winning the event. INSET RIGHT. Maggi, right, and conte Franco Mazzotti, second left, at the Rome grand prix

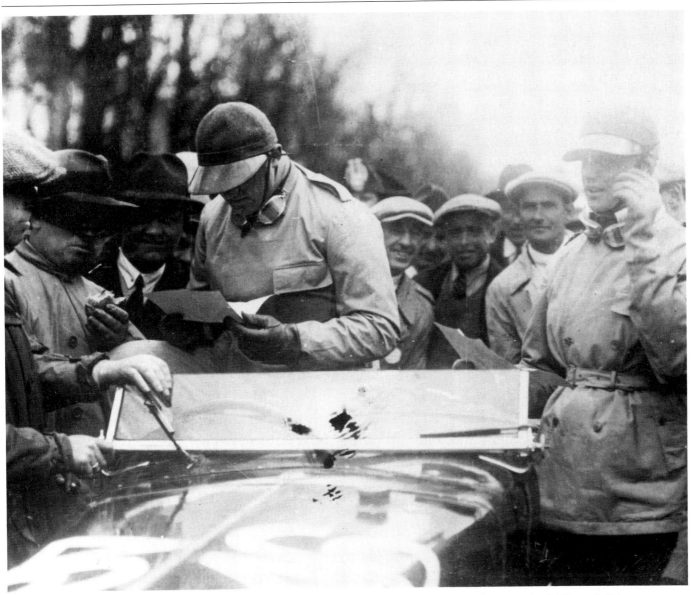

Schoolboy friends conte Aymo Maggi, right, and conte Franco Mazzotti before the start of the 1930 Mille Miglia in which their Alfa Romeo was placed eighth overall. Their finishing time was 17 hours 46 minutes 45 seconds

CONTE MAGGI'S MILLE MIGLIA

Achille Varzi, second right, with conte Aymo Maggi, second left, and their mechanics, after the Spanish grand prix in 1930

The Spanish grand prix at San Sebastian, 1930: Conte Aymo Maggi was second overall to Achille Varzi

CONTE MAGGI'S MILLE MIGLIA

ABOVE, Conte Aymo Maggi (hands on hips) chats with his mechanic before the 1930 Spanish grand prix; and INSET, at the wheel of the Maserati before the start

CONTE MAGGI'S MILLE MIGLIA

Contessa Maggi in 1937

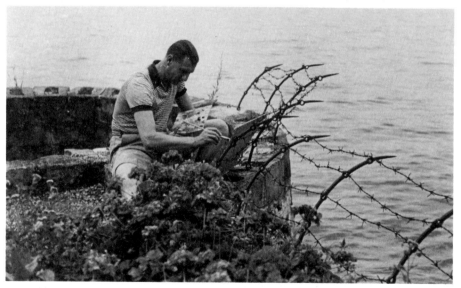

Although he did not consider himself an artist, conte Aymo Maggi loved painting and is seen here on holiday at lake Carezza in August 1938 capturing the scene

Charming and courteous, Maggi would first listen attentively to the subject under discussion, then give a brief, considered judgement in his loud, rough Brescian voice.

Throughout his many years as lord of the manor at Gradella and Calino Maggi was immensely popular with his 'family', as he liked to call them, and he was very knowledgable in all agricultural and farming matters. He was always interested in new production methods and also in improving the wage structure and living conditions of his estate-workers. Every new mayor elected to office could be sure of a friendly summons up to Casa Maggi to make himself and his feelings known, and many churches, youth centres, playing fields and schools received anonymous grants over the years. Maggi loved encouraging sport with the local children and sponsored his own Camillo Maggi football team — named in memory of his younger brother — whose results he followed closely.

Although Great Britain declared war on Nazi Germany on 3 September 1939, Italy and Great Britain were not at war until 10 June 1940, by which time Germany had already invaded Poland, Denmark, Norway, Holland, France, Belgium and Luxembourg. The Dutch, Belgians and Norwegians had capitulated and Dunkirk had been evacuated. It is incredible, therefore, that the thirteenth Mille Miglia was still able to be held on 28 April 1940 on a closed triangular Brescia–Cremona–Mantua–Brescia circuit, victory going to the BMW of Baron Huschke von Hanstein, whose racing overalls bore the notorious SS symbol already feared all over Europe.

When Italy entered the war only six weeks after the race, Maggi joined the crack Vittorio Emanuele Savoia cavalry

The Coppa Ciano, Livorno, March 1939. Conte Aymo Maggi, third left, with senior officers and Giovanni Canestrini, left. The Coppa Ciano was named after Mussolini's son-in-law; BELOW LEFT, having organised the running of the 13th Mille Miglia at the end of April when much of Europe was already occupied, conte Aymo Maggi, now a cavalry officer, Camilla by his side, leaves Brescia station in 1940 to go to war; BELOW RIGHT, conte Aymo Maggi in 1940 at Piedmont on the Franco-Italian frontier during the cold war

regiment as a captain. They were sent to the mountains north of Turin, on the Franco-Italian front, which was then in a state of alertness. At the end of 1940 Maggi's unit, without its horses and now a mechanised regiment, was sent south to Gaeta, between Rome and Naples. There, in idyllic coastal surroundings, they guarded with machine guns the northern approaches to the strategically-important gulf of Gaeta.

It was while at Gaeta that Maggi, who had been troubled with severe stomach spasms for some time, telephoned contessa Camilla to say that he could not stand the pain any more; she arranged to meet him urgently at a consultant surgeon's office in Rome. The surgeon immediately diagnosed acute ulcers on the lower intestine, but he would not operate and sent him on five days sick-leave to the military hospital in Brescia. After this brief stay, Maggi was given a further two months leave, but he was so ill that he never returned to his regiment and was invalided out of the army in 1941. After recuperating in San Remo, he returned home to Calino, Gradella having been taken over by the German High Command.

It was during the winter of 1941–2 that Maggi's childhood friend, Mazzotti, was killed at the age of thirty-eight. He was on active service as a pilot in the Italian airforce as commanding officer of a special combat group, *capo dell'ufficio Comando*, with the 1st Aeriel Zone when his aircraft disappeared on a flight from Tunisia to Sicily. A brief notice issued by his headquarters said that he was believed to have been shot down by a British fighter, but mystery surrounds his death and there was speculation that he had been on a secret mission. The news that Mazzotti was missing in action was announced at a concert in the Teatro

CONTE MAGGI'S MILLE MIGLIA

Conte Aymo Maggi at Calino; BELOW, Calino and its surrounding vineyards

Maggi's regiment moved south in 1941 to guard the gulf of Gaeta between Rome and Naples. He is seen here, LEFT, at Formia in September 1941, shortly before being invalided out of the army because of serious stomach ulcers

Grande in Brescia. The performance was interrupted by the theatre's director, who walked onto the stage carrying a large card and requested one minute's silence in Mazzotti's honour. The audience was stunned, for Mazzotti was an immensely popular public figure, idolised for his exploits as a racing driver, speedboat champion and as a record-breaking airman.

At Calino, country life continued almost as usual, despite shortage of petrol (although as an agricultural landowner, Maggi was allowed a small ration) tyres and cooking oil and the fact that many of the estate-workers had been enlisted in the forces. There were no German troops in the immediate vicinity and on

their infrequent visits to check Casa Maggi and its outbuildings for British airmen, or escaped prisoners, the dust from their staff cars could be seen for miles. Consequently, contessa Camilla had no trouble hiding men in the fields, or up in the haylofts. Maize, rice, bread and vegetables were still plentiful and there were always game and rabbits to be shot for the pot. With its many salons, bedrooms and suites, Casa Maggi would seem an ideal headquarters for the German army, but the tiny white-painted church of San Stefano, at the top of a nearby hill, directly overlooked its gravelled courtyards several hundred feet below. Any German general leaving the safety of the house to step into his

vehicle, would momentarily have been a target for a hungry sniper.

The war dragged on through 1943 and 1944 without too much interruption. Maggi tried to keep the estate going at Calino as usual, but found that Gradella had been left in a sorry state by the retreating Germans. Then in April 1945 the whole village of Calino was filled with tanks and trucks with the arrival of American soldiers throwing out handfuls of candy and cigarettes in return for flagons of Franciacorta wine and clean laundry. The war was over and life on the estates returned to normal.

Maggi's father, Berardo, had been responsible for the renaissance of the Franciacorta wine in the vineyards

44   The Man who Loved Life

The Mille Miglia 1935 poster (*Automobile Club di Brescia*)

surrounding Calino – whose very name *calinos* is Greek for 'dry, arid land' – through his friendship with Father Bonsignori, founder of Remeddo agricultural college, who gave him much practical information about the best types of vine and how they should be cultivated. Maggi made further improvements to the wine but it was the contessa Camilla who, after his death, revitalised the whole wine-making process, installing giant storage vats and modern bottling equipment, which resulted in an expanding production of white, red and spumante wines both for Italian consumption and for export.

In 1947 the Mille Miglia was run again, and there were eleven post-war events. When the race was banned in 1957 after Fon de Portago's Ferrari cart-wheeled into the crowd at Guidizzolo, Maggi's health declined rapidly and he seemed to lose the will to live. Throughout his life he had always enjoyed gambling and in his later years he made several trips with friends to the casino at Monte Carlo. In 1959, on his way back to Gradella from the south of France, he suffered a bad heart attack, but appeared to make a full recovery; two years later, however, he had a second attack at Calino and died there in the house he loved on 23 October 1961. He was fifty-eight.

The conte and contessa Maggi always welcomed overseas entrants at Casa Maggi, Calino, near Brescia, during preparation for the Mille Miglia. Seen here in 1950 the factory team of Jaguar XK120s is unloaded (*Neil Eason-Gibson*)

3 BRESCIAN PIONEERS

Conte Maggi's Mille Miglia played a significant part in Italian motor racing history between 1927 and 1957. But, before looking at the great tradition of the race, one must first establish why it came into being. Why *is* Brescia so steeped in its heritage of road and track, and why has it produced so many enthusiastic sportsmen and brilliant drivers, such as conte Aymo Maggi, Ferdinando Minoia, Giuseppi Morandi and Archimede Rosa? Has its geographical location helped to forge its destiny?

The province of Brescia in the region of Lombardy is most favourably placed in the middle of the Po valley and since prehistoric times has been the focus of many commercial and cultural activities. The first settlement of *Brixia*, from which Brescia got its name, was built on the hill of Cidneo during the late Bronze Age. Emperor Augustus named it *Colonia Civica Augusta Brixia* and provided the city with gates, walls and an aqueduct. Over the centuries it became famous for bronze sculpture, and skilled stone-masons working in marble, and after Brescia came under rule of Venice in 1797, silk and wool production became thriving industries. There had been rich iron deposits in the *valle Trompia*, the lost

Three of the early Brescia 'Settimana' posters (*Automobile Club di Brescia*)

Bruno Boni, centre, mayor of Brescia and great supporter of the Mille Miglia, with conte Aymo Maggi, left, and conte Carlo Castelbarco in Paris for the French prizegiving of 1954 Mille Miglia trophies

valley, at the end of lake Iseo since Roman times, and Brescia was well-known for the manufacturing of superb armour, firearms and weapons; and the centuries-old Beretta dynasty is still known all over the world today.

Brescia is within easy distance of the other Italian lakes, with the industrial cities

Conte Aymo Maggi always prided himself on being a 'bresciano' and was never happier than when in the company of those many Brescian drivers who competed in his own Mille Miglia. He is seen here in 1953 at the prize-giving party in their honour

'horseless carriages' seen on the streets of Brescia was steadily increasing, and he sensed that soon there would be sufficient interest to stage motoring events. Using all his flair and organising ability, Minetti persuaded the owners of every motor-tricycle and automobile in the Brescia area to loan them to him for a limited period – there were twenty of them in all – and in 1896 he promoted the first Brescia Motor Show at the viale Rebuffone Salon. Thousands flocked to see it and Minetti's name was made. That same year he organised his first motor race on a triangular Brescia-Cremona-Peschiera-Brescia circuit, with equal acclaim. His promotional skill was quickly recognised and in 1897 he was invited to stage the third Cycle and Automobile Salon in Milan, and this was both popular and a financial success.

In 1900, Minetti organised the Riunione di Brescia, a 137-mile endurance race, and in 1901 he promoted the 1,000-mile Giro d'Italia cycle race. Later that year he was invited to stage the first Motor Show, at Milan, which set the pattern for all future automobile exhibitions in Europe, and he then took up a senior position with the TCI, the Italian Cycle Touring Club. His original brief was to promote cycle touring holidays, but for the next nine years, as the use of motor cars rapidly increased, he was responsible for the publication of accurate tourist guides and information concerning fuel supplies all over Italy. In those early days it was hazardous to drive long distances in unproven 'horseless carriages' and Minetti laid the groundwork for the national motoring organisations which were to follow. When in 1910 he left the TSI to join Pirelli Tyres as its commercial director, it had lost the grass-roots image it had when it only catered for two-wheeled transport, and

of Milan and Turin to the west; Verona, Vicenza, Padua and Venice to the east; Bergamo, Trento and the Dolomites to the north; and Mantua, Modena and Bologna to the south. Recognising its ideal location, one must now go back sixty years before the Mille Miglia was created, to the year 1866, when Enrico Minetti was born at Nave, north of Brescia. His family had moved to Brescia when he was young and on leaving school he became a successful political journalist. He was also a keen amateur sportsman, not only as a competitor, but as an organiser of events. Minetti loved to organise people, and particularly those who excelled in sport, and he

became the forerunner of a succession of talented Brescian sports promoters such as conte Orazio Oldofredi, Arturo Mercanti and Renzo Castagneto.

Minetti's first venture was to promote cycle races, and in the late 1880s he staged events on a dirt track for such cycling giants as Buni, Pasta, Moreschi, Cittadini, Tomaselli and Pasino. Then, risking everything, he launched his own newspaper, *Il Velocipede*. Originally intended to publicise his own cycle races, this soon became Italy's best-known cycling newspaper.

At the same time as Minetti was staging his races and improving his publication, interest in the intriguing new

Professor Boni has spent a lifetime as a leading representative of Brescian public affairs: for thirty years mayor, he then became President of the Chamber of Commerce and now promotes the new Mille Miglia with the same interest as he had in helping the original races which he loved so much.

Bruno Boni, centre, mayor of Brescia for thirty years, with conte Aymo Maggi, right, and journalist Giovanni Canestrini

Contessa Camilla Maggi welcomes Bruno Boni to Casa Maggi, Calino for the prizegiving to Brescian drivers after the 1956 Mille Miglia

Piero Taruffi and Mario Vandelli are flagged away from the starting ramp in 1952 by Bruno Boni, with Renzo Castagneto, race director, left, and conte Aymo Maggi, right. Their V12 4100cc Ferrari 340 America failed to finish

Conte Aymo Maggi was certainly one of the most sympathetic and interesting citizens in the whole province. The most striking thing about him, of course, was his passion for motor sport, which he showed as the dedicated founder of the wonderful race of the Automobile Club of Brescia (of which I was a vice-president from its inception), in his outstanding ability as a racing driver and in his determined participation in his own event. He was a most colourful personality, not only in Italy, but all over the world. But in describing Aymo it is hard to portray his really individual personality. At first perhaps he appeared rather tough and restless, his gruff voice like a mountain brook running over pebbles, but when one got to know him one could see his extraordinary common

PROFESSOR BRUNO BONI

sense, the warmth of his friendship and his sheer exuberance for life.

He was a victorious driver, who always put real courage into his winning efforts. But I remember him most as the man who brought prestige to our lovely and ancient city when, with conte Franco Mazzotti, sadly lost in a war time action as a pilot over the Mediterranean, the unforgettable Renzo Castagneto and our journalist friend Giovanni Canestrini, he had the idea of creating the Mille Miglia.

His lifelong friendship with Castagneto was wonderful to see. It was based on years of shared experiences and it was a warm and very human relationship, full of co-operation and respect. Shortly after each year's Mille Miglia there would be a full enquiry into the race, when every aspect of its detailed and complex administration, often including the services of at least thirty different civic regions all over Italy, was examined. It would be praised or criticised without bias or rancour. Renzo, in his good-natured and diplomatic way, had the ability to make Aymo see exactly what was needed to improve the race the following year and a long report would be circulated. The result was even closer liaison in the event that they had both created.

Aymo was a man of immense energy and sincerity, and as well known abroad as he was in Brescia. I accompanied him on several occasions when he went on his goodwill missions, giving publicity talks and showing films about the Mille Miglia in many countries. We invariably returned to Brescia with definite promises of the participation of more foreign teams the following year. Then there was his famous hospitality and that of the contessa Camilla, which was really like something from another age. On the eve of the race, everybody who was anybody in the world of motor racing met the civic authorities, the police and the race administrators at the Casa Maggi for a spectacular evening where the talk was only

Bruno Boni, left, before the start of the 1987 Mille Miglia for historic cars with Italian ace Gigi Villoresi, winner of the 1951 race (*Foto Eden*)

Conte Giovanni Lurani, right, veteran of nine Mille Miglias, before the 1987 event with Bruno Boni, now president of the Brescian Chamber of Commerce (*Foto Eden*)

of the Mille Miglia and the great champions of the past.

But these were not Aymo's only characteristics. Anyone who knew him could not fail to be captivated by his charm, his sense of humour and his courage – for at the end of the war he was a sick man, plagued by painful and recurring stomach ulcers – but nothing could divert him from his chosen path.

To understand what the man was really like one must consider that fateful Mille Miglia of 1947, and I feel honoured to have played my part in working so closely with

him then. I was deeply involved with the political aspect of trying to re-introduce a major sporting event so soon after the war and knew the problems that we faced. It wasn't like staging a one-off sporting promotion in one particular location, say an international football match or an athletics meeting, where everyone would be under the same roof. We were trying to get the Mille Miglia back to its former glory along a 1,000 mile route littered with pot-holed roads, broken bridges and tangled communications, and a punishing restriction of tyre and petrol to put our pre-war cars into condition for such a hazardous undertaking.

Despite criticism – and this came from the highest level at times – Aymo shrugged aside every obstacle with his sheer persuasion, grim determination and occasional outburst of authority, which he would display when he thought necessary: a case of the iron hand in the velvet glove. I remember being present at a meeting at the family estate with senior civic officials from Brescia and other provinces through which the race would run. At first they were like broken men, full of pessimism, some even set against running the Mille Miglia again. But after listening to their difficulties, Aymo was able to reassure them and they went away happy, for the endearing nobleman had understood their needs and convinced them that their problems could be overcome.

Now nearly thirty years after his death, it still does not seem possible that this tall, elegant nobleman of charm and dignity has really gone from our lives and that we will never see that cheery wave again. Like all of us in Brescia, I will always remember our favourite citizen, who through the famous red arrow symbol of the Mille Miglia spread our city's fame around the world. When Aymo Maggi died his own crusade was over and it had been fought with the same courage and devotion as shown by his ancestor more than seven hundred years before.

CONTE MAGGI'S MILLE MIGLIA

An early shot of the old Brescian cycle track, with Renzo Castagneto, right, who later became race director of the Mille Miglia

now covered all forms of transport, including the expanding field of aviation.

In the fifteen years between 1895 and 1910, Minetti showed that he was a man of foresight and determination and as his fame as an organiser increased, so did the excellence of his promotions. In 1904, with Arturo Mercanti, another well-known sports promoter and entrepreneur, he promoted the second Riunione di Brescia, a 205-mile race for the Coppa d'Italia, and in September 1905 the first of the *Settimana Automobilistica*

Bresciana, the Brescia Speed Weeks, where the first circuit of Brescia for the Coppa Florio was run over 300 miles of the old Brescia circuit. It was won by Vincenzo Lancia at 72 mph, with third place going to conte Vincenzo Florio himself (Mercedes). In 1906 Florio staged his own race for the first time on the old Madonie circuit outside Palermo; the Targa Florio, or 'Florio's Plate', named after the solid gold plate he commissioned from a Parisian goldsmith as a prize.

In 1911, the year after he had joined Pirelli, Minetti left to form a thriving distributorship for Lancia cars with his friend Vincenzo Lancia who had stopped racing in 1908. Others followed in his footsteps, but Enrico Minetti will always be remembered as the man who brought motor shows, cycling, motor-cycling and motor racing, aircraft and balloon racing, circus, live theatre and equestrian events to the people of Brescia.

After the end of World War I in 1918, Europe returned painfully to normality; the

The poster for the first Italian grand prix held in Brescia in 1921. This was the race that Arturo Mercanti 'stole' to Monza the following year (*Automobile Club di Brescia*)

Conte Aymo Maggi, right, with Rino Berardi, left, before the start of the Monza grand prix (Bugatti), with race officials

major Italian races between 1919 and 1921 were the Targa Florio, the circuit of Montenero at Leghorn and the circuit of Mugello at Florence. In 1921, a new grand prix formula for 3000 cc cars was introduced and the Automobile Club of Milan staged the first Italian grand prix on the Fascia d'Oro circuit at Brescia; it was won by the Frenchman Jules Goux (Ballot), who averaged 89 mph for the 322 miles.

The Brescia grand prix week was watched by huge crowds, many tempted by concessionary train fares from Milan, and front-page headlines proclaimed the 'Resounding Success of Brescia's Super-circuit', but sinister moves were going on behind the scenes. Arturo Mercanti, who though he lived in Brescia had not been born there, had already made arrangements with officials of the Automobile Club in Milan to rush through the construction of a new autodrome circuit in the Parco Reale at Monza, outside Milan, with himself as director of the syndicate. Perhaps jealous of Brescia's long string of motoring firsts, the club used its considerable influence to have the grand prix taken away and in September 1922 it was held for the first time at Monza.

Although it is said that the people of Brescia never forgave Mercanti for 'stealing' their race just twelve months after their own running of the Italian grand prix had been so successful, this bitterness obviously did not affect the race directors of the Mille Miglia. Mercanti's entry was never barred diplomatically and he actually finished six Mille Miglias in succession from the debut in 1927 to 1932, driving an Alfa Romeo under the pseudonym of '*Frate Ignoto*', the 'unknown monk'.

Mercanti and Minetti had considerable influence on Lombardy's motor racing scene, sowing the first seeds of competition at the turn of the century, but brief reference must also be made to such talented Brescian drivers as conte Aymo Maggi, Ferdinando Minoia, Guiseppi Morandi and Archimede Rosa. All were of the highest calibre and capable of winning races against the

CONTE MAGGI'S MILLE MIGLIA

The Coppa Acerbo in 1924: Crowded pit road before the start

Conte Aymo Maggi winning the 1926 Coppa Etna in Sicily in stark surroundings (Bugatti)

best of their day. Finally, there is the significant contribution made by the sturdy and reliable OM cars from the Officine Meccaniche in Brescia under the direction of Signor Orazi and chief engineer Fuscaldo, who had had considerable experience with Fiat, Nazzaro and Zust cars. In 1926 an OM won the coveted Rudge-Whitworth Biennial Cup in the Le Mans twenty-four hour race and a strong team of three factory cars was entered in the first Mille Miglia in 1927, driven by Minoia/Morandi;

T. Danieli/Balestrero; M. Danieli/Rosa.
    Ferdinando 'Nando' Minoia was already an established ace, having won the Coppa Florio on the Brescia circuit in 1907 in his Isotta Fraschini and enjoying many successes with Taunus, Lorraine-Dietrich, Benz and Alfa Romeo. Morandi had grand prix experience and had often ridden with Minoia, and the Danieli brothers were steady and reliable. Renato Balestrero also had a good record in circuit races and Rosa was a superb test driver at the OM factory. The

Conte Aymo Maggi in his Bugatti on the front row of the grid at the 1924 Coppa Acerbo

Conte Aymo Maggi in the Alfa Romeo before winning the Coppa Messina, Sicily, in 1926

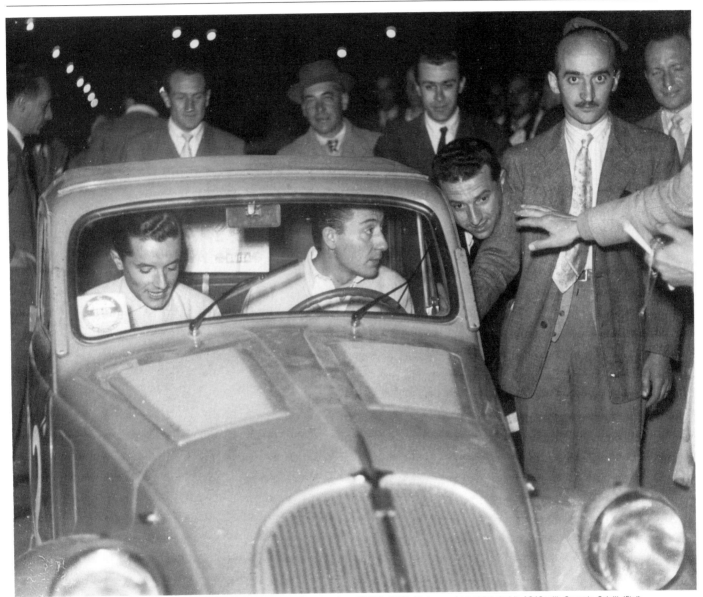

Brescian driver Guido Berlucchi, left, completed the Mille Miglia for six consecutive years from 1949 to 1954. He is seen here at the start in 1949 with Gregorio Celotti (Fiat). They finished the race in 21 hours 58 minutes (*Guido Berlucchi*)

CONTE MAGGI'S MILLE MIGLIA

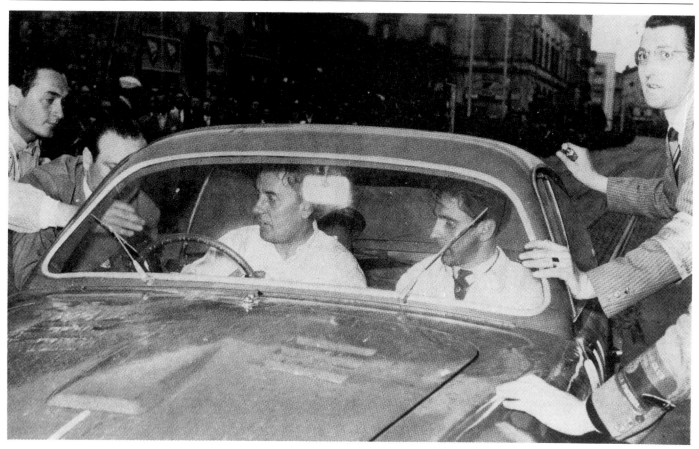

Giovanni Bracco and Alfonso Rolfo in their Ferrari
225S during the 1952 Mille Miglia. They are seen here
at the Siena control en route to a fine victory

Conte Aymo Maggi presenting the
prizes for Brescian drivers at the
Automobile Club following the 20th
Mille Miglia in 1953. Note the wall
poster, which confirms that the
race was watched by 16 million

From the first Mille Miglia in 1927, the piazza Vittoria, Brescia, was the centre of attraction during race week. It was here that all competing cars were scrutineered in the days before the start. This overhead shot from 1950 shows the enthusiasm and clamour of the spectators and the famous 'red arrow' symbol of the Mille Miglia (*Neil Eason-Gibson*)

CONTE MAGGI'S MILLE MIGLIA

team was expected to do well, but they swept the board with the 6-cylinder 2-litre Superba models, finishing first, second and third overall, led by the Nando Minoia/Giuseppi Morandi car in just under 21 hours and 5 minutes.

The sporting and technical achievements of the OM team were considerable and for weeks after the Mille Miglia the team was fêted on an extended promotional tour which took the victorious cars and drivers all over Italy. The first Mille Miglia had proved that Italian cars and drivers were capable of winning against leading opposition, but most of all it showed the way ahead for future races. The Mille Miglia was obviously not a race in which to be driving a perfectly standard, series production car without any special preparation, for those were the vehicles that dropped out. It was obvious that to be successful a car would have to be very carefully prepared and incorporate the finest possible material and parts.

But OM's successes were to continue, for in 1928 they were second (Rosa/ Mazzotti), in 1929 second and fifth (Morandi/Rosa and Ghersi/Guerrini), in 1930 fifth (Bassi/Gazzabini) and in 1931 were third again (Morandi/Rosa). The increased power and reliability of the Alfa Romeos finally forced OM out of the record books, but their influence in the early Mille Miglias did much to enhance Brescia's rekindled passion for motor sport.

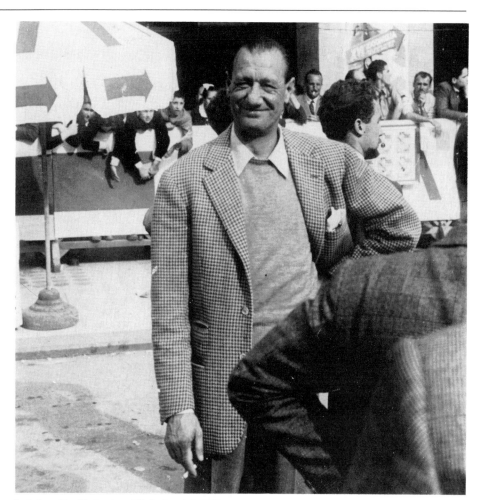

Conte Aymo Maggi in the piazza Vittoria, Brescia in 1951

4 | CONTE MAGGI'S RACING AND THE MILLE MIGLIA

'To win the Mille Miglia was the proudest moment of my life.'

PIERO TARUFFI

Conte Aymo Maggi gave up motor-cycle racing in 1922 to concentrate on motor racing and his first victory was in 1923, driving a Chiribiri in the Ponte decimo-Giovo hillclimb. In 1924 he won the 1500 cc class and was fourth overall in his Bugatti on the circuit of lake Garda. The following year he raced in many international events, mostly in the Bugatti, and won the circuit of Garda outright. He became a good friend of 'le patron' Ettore Bugatti, and took a flat at Molsheim to be near the Bugatti factory. It was at this time that Maggi opened a Bugatti agency in Milan and took on young Rino Berardi as his own racing mechanic and test-driver.

In 1926 with a new Type 35 grand prix Bugatti, Maggi scored a brilliant win in the Rome grand prix and then victories in Sicily, in the Coppa Vinci at Messina and the Coppa Etna at Catania. Bugatti was delighted and offered him a factory drive in the Alsace grand prix at Strasbourg, which was restricted to lightweight 1100 cc cycle-cars. Bugatti entered three cars for Andre Dubonnet, Pierre Vizcaya and Aymo Maggi. Maggi chased Dubonnet, the eventual winner, hard and was annoyed when he was twice flagged down by team manager Bartolomeo Constantini and forced to follow team

An early shot of conte Aymo Maggi at the wheel

1925: Conte Aymo Maggi (Bugatti) after winning his first circuit of lake Garda, watched by his proud father, Berardo, back left

The cobble-stoned circuit through the streets around lake Garda, won by conte Aymo Maggi in both 1925 and 1926 (Bugatti). While Maggi changes plugs, riding mechanic Rino Berardi tightens the front wheel

orders. But he was victorious at lake Garda for a second time and was rated one of Europe's leading racing drivers. He then won the Nave-San Eusebio hillclimb, and it was while returning to Brescia that Maggi came up with the idea of a rough road race for sports cars to get Italian motor sport and the automobile industry out of its deep depression.

After the foundation of the Mille Miglia in December 1926, there was considerable criticism and even scepticism from some sectors of the motoring and national press about the average speed of 45 mph which Maggi forecast could be maintained over 1,000 miles. The thought of racing round Italy on open roads in a single stage event caused the authorities to flinch and, Castagneto remembers, gave everyone

Conte Aymo Maggi (Bugatti) winning the circuit of lake Garda in 1926 for the second successive year with Rino Berardi

except Aymo nagging doubts from time to time. 'But he overcame every obstacle and the first Mille Miglia was run on 26–27 March 1927. Aymo was a real sportsman and a fierce competitor and in order to overcome the initial criticism he himself drove a massive 7-litre Isotta Fraschini the whole 1,000 miles to finish sixth overall in 22 hours.'

Maggi's co-driver was his friend Bindo Maserati, one of the four Maserati brothers, who were known as battery and sparking-plug manufacturers and later builders of Maserati cars. After eleven stops for fuel and three to change tyres – one third of that year's route was on dirt roads – they returned triumphantly in exactly 22 hours 35 seconds in sixth

place overall and winner of the 8000 cc class. Overall race winners Ferdinando Minoia and Guiseppi Morandi, Brescian drivers driving a Brescia-built OM, averaged 48 mph, even faster than Maggi's estimate. Publicity from the first race was enormous, its critics were silenced overnight, and the Mille Miglia was set on its historic path.

Conte Aymo Maggi, left with his Maserati before winning the Coppa Messina at Caserta, Sicily, in 1926

Alfieri Maserati at the wheel of his own Maserati car during the Targa Florio, 1927, when he finished third. In this race Conte Guilio Masetti, twice winner of the race, was killed when his Delage overturned. Conte Aymo Maggi's Maserati retired with a broken chassis

Crowds line the circuit at the finish of the Targa Florio in 1927

Later that year, Maggi drove another fine race on the circuit of Garda. Going for his third win, he was leading Tazio Nuvolari on the final lap when a tyre burst and he went out within sight of the finish, letting the 'Flying Mantuan' through to victory. After the first successful Mille Miglia in 1927, Maggi found he became increasingly involved with its administration and promotion and he was reluctantly forced to cut down on his own racing programme.

He failed to finish in the 1928 Mille Miglia driving with Ernesto Maserati, though he came second in the circuit of Pozzo at Verona, and in 1929 he had just one race — the Mille Miglia. Sharing an OM with his old friend conte Franco Mazzotti, they retired with mechanical trouble soon after the start. In 1930,

Maggi's last full season as a driver and at the wheel of an Alfa Romeo, he drove in the Targa Florio with Mazzotti and with Mazzotti again was placed eighth in that year's Mille Miglia, sharing the Brescia grand prix team prize with the Alfa Romeos of Achille Varzi/Carlo Canavesi and Pietro Ghersi/Franco Cortese. Maggi came third in the circuit of Montenero, Leghorn and finished second to team-

Conte Aymo Maggi and Rino Berardi with their Maserati in the 1927 Targa Florio on the Medium Madonie circuit, Sicily. The race distance was 335 miles, in five laps, and one single lap took 90 minutes

Conte Aymo Maggi and Rino Berardi during a pit-stop on the 1927 Targa Florio, before returning their Maserati with a broken chassis. Note the *caribinieri* watching in heavy uniforms despite the April sun

Conte Carlo Masetti, killed on the Targa Florio

Conte Aymo Maggi drove an Alfa Romeo in the Tripoli grand prix on the Mellaha circuit in 1929

mate Varzi in the Spanish grand prix at San Sebastian. In 1933 he drove a Fiat 1100 cc in the Mille Miglia with Ricci, winning the 1100 cc class for production cars.

On 5 April 1936, when the Mille Miglia was run for the tenth time, the involvement of the Italian army in the fierce war in Ethiopia was at its peak and the Mille Miglia was held in an atmosphere of pre-occupied and anxious patriotism. Italy's victory was announced one month after the race.

The race was marred by a raging political argument concerning government regulations and the use of alternative types of petrol to standard pump fuel which was of low octane. It was this low quality fuel which made the oil companies experiment in a blaze of publicity with methanol- and benzol-based fuels, such as Alfa Romeo and Maserati used in their grand prix cars. Certainly the victories of Alfa Romeo in 1934 and 1935 were not gained with standard pump petrol and the 1936 Mille Miglia was full of rancour and dissention. Because of its numerous political problems, the race remained a national event, with twenty-three of the sixty-nine

72

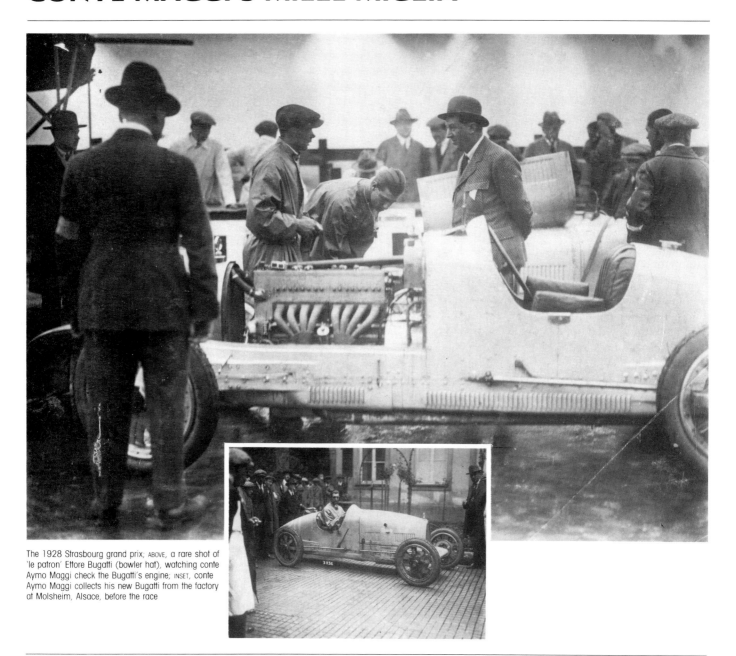

The 1928 Strasbourg grand prix; ABOVE, a rare shot of 'le patron' Ettore Bugatti (bowler hat), watching conte Aymo Maggi check the Bugatti's engine; INSET, conte Aymo Maggi collects his new Bugatti from the factory at Molsheim, Alsace, before the race

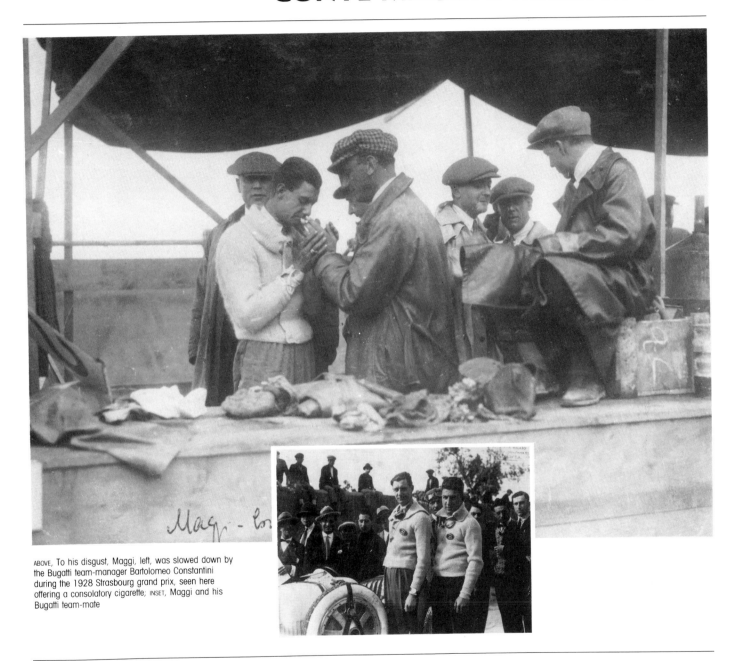

ABOVE, To his disgust, Maggi, left, was slowed down by the Bugatti team-manager Bartolomeo Constantini during the 1928 Strasbourg grand prix, seen here offering a consolatory cigarette; INSET, Maggi and his Bugatti team-mate

Giovanni Canestrini, left, with conte Aymo Maggi

Aymo Maggi was a real prodigy; a true, complete sportsman, who lived in the days when values counted for something. He had no time for false modesty, commercialism or hypocrisy, traits so common in sport today.

The last time I saw him was in the street in Rome, when he embraced me warmly and said, 'dear Giovanni, it seems that time has already passed us by.' He was referring, of course, to the Mille Miglia, to which he had given so much fire, so much passion, so much energy and which was now banned forever. It was a race in which, from the outset, real champions had battled for the supreme victory.

But this Maggi was not the young and courageous driver of a grand prix Bugatti, whom we knew and loved on the circuit of Garda – good-looking, impetuous and with a ready smile. This was the figure of a melancholy man, still young, still full of energy, but seemingly behind the times.

After World War II, Maggi was a representative of the C.S.I. on the sporting commission of the Italian Automobile Club. At the Monza grand prix he was called in to settle a pre-race dispute between entrants over a clause in the race regulations. His terse comment was, 'For me, the sport we love does not need petty quarrels over the rules. In my opinion, the sportsman is the one who sets out and comes back first.' All his life, Maggi followed this principle; whatever he did, he fought for to the best of his ability; second best was not good enough.

This was perhaps why he always wanted Casa Maggi at Calino to be transformed into a dream castle – a citadel – during Mille Miglia race week, so that the drivers, the race officials and all his friends could share his good fortune. A citadel in which he could play the role of the grand seigneur in his own humble way, a nobleman who wanted to share his treasures with the world.

But Maggi's real fame was for creating the Mille Miglia, yet to understand the background of the race, one must remember Brescia's long tradition of motor sport, for they were really pioneers. When the first Italian grand prix was held on the Fascia d'Oro circuit at Brescia in 1921, won by the French Ballots of Jules Goux and J. Chassagne, there was a crisis in the whole automotive industry, not only in Italy, but all over Europe.

Then came the blow we had been dreading: the authorities in Milan were pushing ahead with the construction of a new autodrome circuit at Monza with a syndicate led by the Brescian entrepreneur, Arturo Mercanti. In 1922 the second Italian grand prix was snatched from Brescia and given to Monza.

In the spring of 1925 there was a desolate body of motor sports enthusiasts around Brescia suffering from a general apathy. Then suddenly on 29 March, the situation looked brighter when Maggi won the Rome grand prix (Bugatti) beating the Alfa Romeos of conte Gastone Brilli Peri and Giovanni Bonmartini, and soon afterwards won the Coppa Etna in Sicily. Coupled with Maggi's racing successes, Renato Balestrero, had a fine victory on the Mellaha circuit in Italian north Africa, winning the Tripoli grand prix in a Brescia-built OM. The same marque with its reliable 2000 cc engine later set thirty-six international records at Monza, running non-stop for six days and averaging 65 mph for the 9,375 miles covered. This series of positive results by Brescian cars and drivers set local pulses racing, as a contemporary newspaper cutting reported:

GIOVANNI CANESTRINI

Giovanni Canestrini, right, conte Aymo Maggi, centre, and Renzo Castagneto at the reception for Brescian drivers following the 1953 Mille Miglia

While the activity of sportsmen has been stagnating until the past few days, the fever of sporting enthusiasts has been increasing. European champions, most of whom can only drive for their factory team, would like to show themselves on the larger motor racing stage. The public eagerly awaits the renaissance – but does not know how, or when it will come.

The germ of an idea was beginning to grow and it took form in December 1926 and then spread quickly for two reasons. Firstly because of Maggi's wonderful victory on the circuit of Lake Garda for the second time and then with the announcement of the substantial modifications to the existing grand prix formula for the 1927 season, which put a virtual embargo on those cars and greatly enhanced the sports car scene. In the same year a new grand prix for 'voiturettes' or small cars up to 1500 cc was introduced. Little interest was shown in it and the French grand prix at Mirimas, for which the organisers had expected twenty starters, was a

shambles. Only three cars came to the line – all Bugattis – and only those of Jules Goux and Meo Constantini finished. The Italian grand prix at Monza was no better, this time only the two Bugattis of 'Sabipa', a pseudonym for Charavel, and Constantini being classified. Motor racing in Europe was in a pathetic state and the public was rapidly losing interest.

At that time the Italian state railway was introducing many new services to woo motorists away from the roads and, with arguments raging on both sides, several 'match' races were staged by aces such as Maggi and Achille Varzi. With much newspaper publicity, Maggi set out from Brescia station in his Bugatti sports car and raced the Venice express from Brescia to Milan central station. Varzi wagered the directors of the newly-introduced Pullman service from Milan to San Remo that he could beat the train with a Lancia Lambda. And Maggi and Varzi both just won their bets. Years later, Maggi said to Castegneto: 'Today's so-called sportsmen only discuss starting money and bonuses. At least when we raced

the trains we did it for fun. It's time we did something different again.'

The outcome of the meeting in my apartment with Maggi, Mazzotti and Castagneto in December 1926 is now history and entries for the new race were requested as soon as the Automobile Club of Brescia was opened on 18 January 1927. The original hostility and adverse comments about the intended race by some of the press and non-sporting factions were gradually overcome and there were prospects of millions lining the route for the whole 1,000 miles. The night before the inaugural race on 26 March, nobody had much sleep, neither drivers nor the organisers, as everyone was thinking of the road ahead.

Maggi arrived at the start early, and his bright red Isotta Fraschini bore the number '5' on its sides. He was really happy with the number of entrants and he was the only one of us four founders – the 'four musketeers' – who actually drove in that first Mille Miglia. As Maggi got in the car, just before the start, with his reserve driver and mechanic Bindo Maserati, he commented as always, 'either I get there, or I break it', a habit of his. They did not have an easy task, but from the outset he was determined to tame the wild horses under the bonnet of that fabulous machine. On race day Maggi was still only twenty-three, but he had an exuberance and natural talent that few youngsters before him had ever shown. He had recently completed rigorous military service as a tough and disciplined cavalry officer and he was physically fit and at the peak of his career. With his neat racing overalls, his checked cap and with spare goggles slung around his neck, he greeted the friends and admirers who crowded around the car. Maggi and Maserati returned to Brescia twenty-two hours later, covered in dust but smiling even more broadly as winners of the 8000 cc class and in sixth place overall. That was just the sort of challenge that he enjoyed.

In the Cremona grand prix in 1924 conte Aymo Maggi's Bugatti lapped at 64 mph

starters being Alfa Romeo and twenty-five Fiat Ballila. The only foreign entrant was the 1500 cc Aston Martin which went out of the race near Rome.

The race organisers were also criticised for permitting the entry of six cars of ridiculously small engine capacity, running on coal-gas fuel, or *carbonella*, for experimental use as a political sop. It was said that they had no rightful place in the Mille Miglia, which was won by the Alfa Romeo of Brivio/Ongaro in 13 hours

7 minutes 51 seconds, just 32 seconds ahead of the Farina/Meazza Alfa Romeo, against the fastest of the 'gasogeni', which took a full 31 hours. The three new 8-cylinder Alfa Romeos of Brivio, Farina and in third place Pintacuda/Stefani, were virtually single-seater grand prix cars with stark two-seater bodies (providing a gruelling ride for the travelling mechanic) and with no opposition they dominated the race.

After the austerity of 1936, Italy was in

a state of euphoria with its victory in Ethiopia when the eleventh Mille Miglia was held on 4–5 April 1937, some welcome overseas competition coming from the French. At that time there were no competitive French grand prix cars and so manufacturers like Bugatti, Delage, Delahaye and Talbot concentrated on building sturdy touring cars running without compressors. Delahaye entered works cars for Rene Dreyfus/Pietro Ghersi and Laurie Schell/

78

In the 1933 Mille Miglia MG cars received an invitation from the King of Italy and Benito Mussolini to enter an official team. Three 6-cylinder 1100 cc Magnettes were entered, driven by Lord Howe/Denis Hamilton, Sir Henry Birkin/Bernard Rubin and Captain George Eyston/conte Giovanni Lurani. The Eyston/Lurani car seen here with 'Johnny' Lurani nearest the camera won the 1100 cc class. George Eyston held the land speed record three times in his 'Thunderbolt' car in 1937 and 1938 and acheived 357.50 mph on Bonneville Salt Flats, U.S.A. (*Lurani Archive*)

Refuelling at Imola. Achille Varzi (Alfa Romeo), centre, facing the camera, is advised by Enzo Ferrari to change from dry to wet weather tyres during the 1934 Mille Miglia. Varzi carried on to beat his arch rival Tazio Nuvolari by 8 minutes 53 seconds (*Ferrari Archives*)

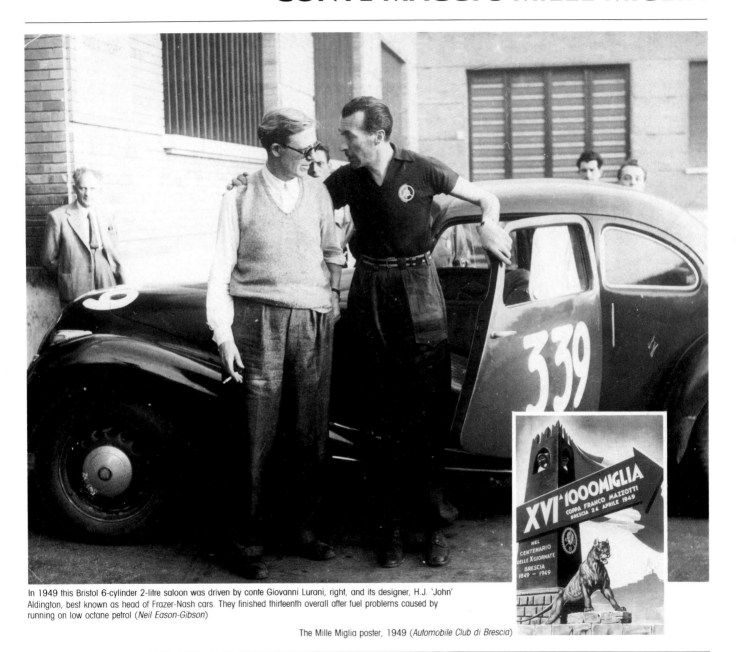

In 1949 this Bristol 6-cylinder 2-litre saloon was driven by conte Giovanni Lurani, right, and its designer, H.J. 'John' Aldington, best known as head of Frazer-Nash cars. They finished thirteenth overall after fuel problems caused by running on low octane petrol (*Neil Eason-Gibson*)

The Mille Miglia poster, 1949 (*Automobile Club di Brescia*)

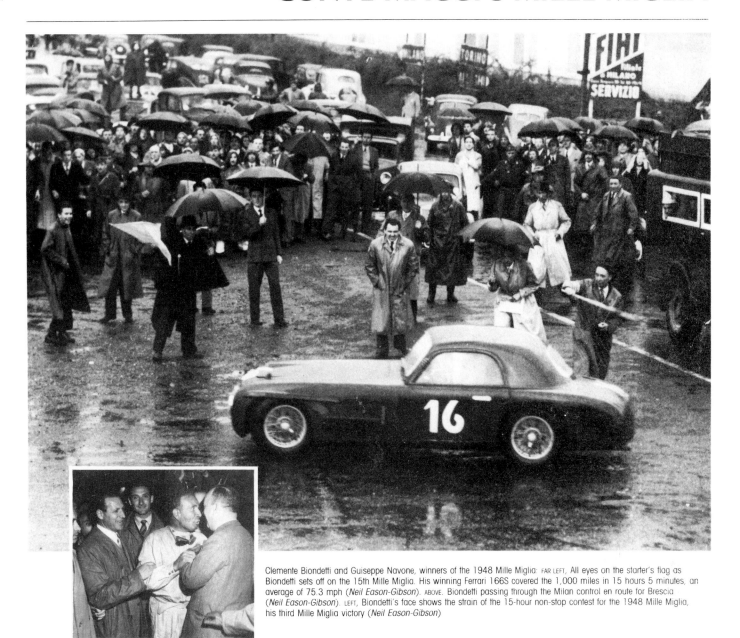

Clemente Biondetti and Guiseppe Navone, winners of the 1948 Mille Miglia: FAR LEFT, All eyes on the starter's flag as Biondetti sets off on the 15th Mille Miglia. His winning Ferrari 166S covered the 1,000 miles in 15 hours 5 minutes, an average of 75.3 mph (*Neil Eason-Gibson*). ABOVE, Biondetti passing through the Milan control en route for Brescia (*Neil Eason-Gibson*). LEFT, Biondetti's face shows the strain of the 15-hour non-stop contest for the 1948 Mille Miglia, his third Mille Miglia victory (*Neil Eason-Gibson*)

Clemente Biondetti was again winner of the Mille Miglia in 1949 in the Ferrari Tipo 166MM with Ettore Salani and is given the chequered flag by Renzo Castagneto (*Giannino Marzotto*)

Carrière and the Talbot factory at Suresnes had cars for Cattaneo/Lavegue and Comotti/Archimede Rosa.

An entirely new Alfa Romeo 2300 cc B model was the property of 'Il Duce' Benito Mussolini and had been fitted with a superb saloon body built by the coachbuilders Touring of Milan. It was entered in the programme simply as 'Boratto/ G. B. Guidotti', Boratto being none other than Mussolini's chauffeur. It

was Gianbattista Guidotti, the famous Alfa Romeo *collaudatori*, or test-driver, who drove the entire race to finish fourth overall in 15 hours 40 minutes, but all the glory went to Mussolini's chauffeur. In addition to this win of the 1500 cc National Touring class, Mussolini's eldest son, Vittorio drove well in a Fiat 1500 cc, helping his Scuderia Parioli win the Brescia grand prix prize for the best three-car team.

The twelfth Mille Miglia, run on 3 April 1938 in perfect weather, was won by the Alfa Romeo of Biondetti/Stefani, the first of Biondetti's four Mille Miglia victories, in a record time which was to remain unbroken for fifteen years. It was the last of the classic pre-war races. Several route changes ensured an ultra-fast race and the redoubtable Biondetti from Tuscany, driving the new 8-cylinder 3000 cc Alfa Romeo with twin compressors,

Tazio Nuvolari, 'the flying mantuan', left, who did so much to popularise the sport of motor racing with the Italian public, with conte Aymo Maggi

actually used the same motor as a Type 308 grand prix car. He became the first to complete the 1,000 miles in under twelve hours, averaging nearly 85 mph.

The 1938 event was marred, however, by an accident to one of the smaller and potentially safer saloon cars. Just after leaving the Bologna control a Lancia Aprilia, driven by amateurs from Genoa, Bruzzo and Mignanego, somersaulted into the crowd after crossing a tram-line; it killed ten spectators outright, including seven children, and seriously injured twenty-three others. Whether the accident was caused by mechanical failure or human error was never established, but the following day the Italian government banned the Mille Miglia from racing on public roads in built-up areas. It was difficult to see how it could ever be run again.

The ban was still effective in 1939 and no race was held. However, late that year, with war-clouds threatening, Maggi made a top-level historic journey to Berlin with Mazzotti and Renzo Castagneto in order to persuade the Nazi high command and senior German automotive executives at the Berlin Motor Show to send a strong team of BMW cars to enter an amended Mille Miglia to be run on 28 April 1940. Castagneto recalled:

I always remember how Maggi would travel anywhere at any time to draw attention to his cause and that journey to Berlin late in 1939 is vividly clear. After suspension of the race in 1938 following a serious accident involving crowd fatalities, we received permission to run a modified Mille Miglia on a triangular Brescia-Cremona-Mantua-Brescia circuit in 1940. With war looming it

CONTE MAGGI'S MILLE MIGLIA

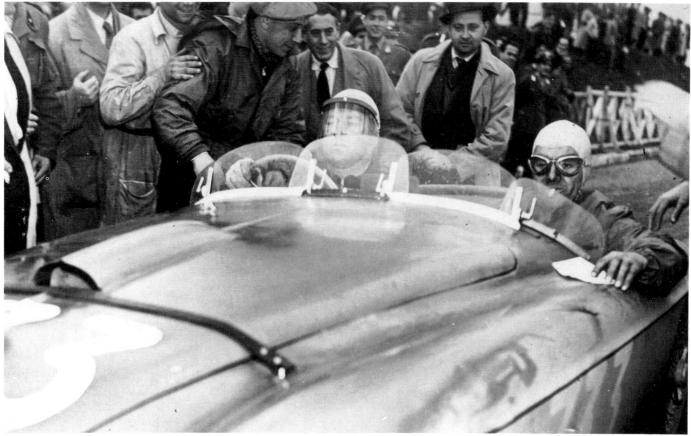

The second-placed Ferrari 195S of Dorino Serafini and Ettore Salani at a passage control during the 1950 Mille Miglia. As Serafini accelerates away, Salani still awaits the Automobile Club stamp to prove they have checked through that control (*Neil Eason-Gibson*)

was obvious this was likely to be only a national event unless we could be guaranteed the entry of a strong foreign team. Knowing that senior executives of the German automobile industry would be gathered at the Berlin Motor Show in December, Maggi decided that he, Mazzotti and I should go there to promote our interest in the race. We left Brescia at 10 a.m. and arrived in Berlin at midnight, after an exhausting drive, to find every hotel booked solid because of the Salon. But the journey was well worthwhile for we returned to Brescia with the promise of a strong BMW factory team. This meant that we could promote the thirteenth Mille Miglia — or the First Gran Premio Brescia delle Mille Miglia — as an international event. Victory went to the Baron Huschke von Hanstein/Walter Baumer BMW with other BMW cars in third, fifth and sixth places. Shortly afterwards Italy was also at war and all sporting activity finished.

The lap distance in this thirteenth Mille Miglia was 167 km (103 miles) and it had

A classic shot of Baron Huschke von Hanstein, right, after winning the 1940 wartime Mille Miglia with Walter Baumer. Note the SS emblem on his racing overalls. After the war he became race director of Porsche (*Ferrari Archives*)

CONTE MAGGI'S MILLE MIGLIA

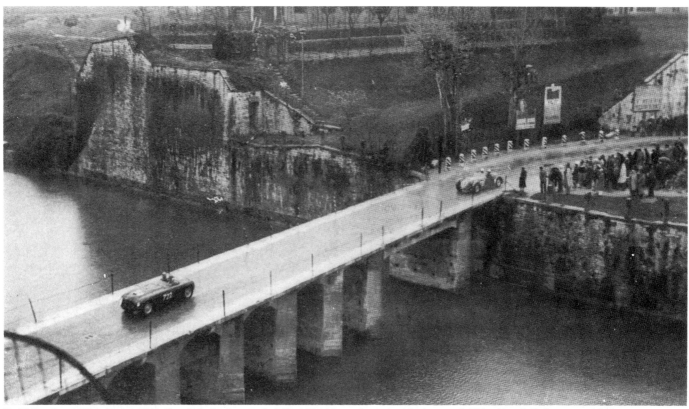

The 2340 cc Ferrari 195S, driven by Vittorio Marzotto/Fontana, crosses the bridge at Peschiera on its way to ninth place overall. All four Marzotto brothers, sons of Conte Marzotto of textile dynasty, drove Ferraris in the 1950 race, which was won by Giannino Marzotto with Crosara. They won again in 1953. Brescia-born driver Aldo Bassi was killed that year when his Ferrarri crashed heavily in the rain; English driver Monkhouse died after his Healey went off the road, and the Italian lorda was killed in an horrific crash near Désenzano. *Autocar* called the race `1,000 desperate miles' (*Giannino Marzotto*)

to be covered nine times. Original thoughts that the event would be held in Libya – as a Tobruk to Tripoli race for example – were rejected. The circuit was identical to the one used in Brescia in 1905, with the addition of specially-built link roads to ensure that town centres were eliminated, and the superbly-prepared Touring-bodied saloon of von Hanstein/Baumer won in 8 hours 54 minutes at an average of 103 mph.

But it was a ludicrous situation: Germany had already invaded Poland, Norway and France and yet the entire BMW entourage and French teams stayed in adjacent rooms at the Hotel Vittoria in Brescia – and Englishman, William Bradley, the doyen of motoring journalists, attended the race without being arrested. Von Hanstein, the bespectacled driver of the winning BMW, wore white overalls bearing the streaked lightning

emblem of the SS; he later became director of Porsche. Italy was then adopting its non-aggression policy and did not declare war on England until six weeks later.

The thirteenth Mille Miglia was the last until after World War II and during that time Italy underwent catastrophic changes. Although things seemed comparatively easy in the early stages of the war, the situation altered rapidly after

Clemente Biondetti, 'King of the Mille Miglia', who won the race in 1938, 1947, 1948 and 1949 and was fourth in 1940 and 1954: a proud *Tuscano*, he is seen here after his 1949 victory with Ettore Salani (*Neil Eason-Gibson*)

CONTE MAGGI'S MILLE MIGLIA

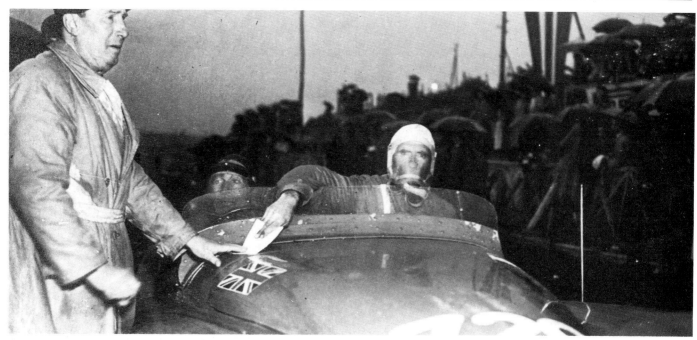

After four victories, Clemente Biondetti switched from Ferrari to Jaguar in 1950, but the British car failed to give him a fifth. ABOVE, Biondetti and Gino Bronzoni leave the Rome control on their way to eighth place overall (*Neil Eason-Gibson*). BELOW, Biondetti at Casa Maggi, Calino in 1950 while preparing for the Mille Miglia (*Neil Eason-Gibson*)

Sicily fell and the Italian mainland was invaded by the allied forces with devastating effect. When the war ended in May 1945 the country's entire communications network was wrecked, hundreds of bridges had been destroyed and thousands of miles of roads and railways were pot-holed and twisted rubble. Maggi, his race director Castagneto and their old friend Bruno Boni, the long-serving mayor of Brescia and friend of the Mille Miglia, plotted desperately to reinstate the race, but it was impossible to achieve in 1946. Later that year, however, Maggi drove in his penultimate competitive event, the Nave-San Eusebio hillclimb, which he won in his Alfa Romeo and also set the fastest lap.

Persuasion and perserverence eventually succeeded however and on 21–22 June 1947, the first post-war Mille Miglia, the fourteenth event, was run over 1,139 miles. There were 155 starters and 54 finishers, victory going to the Romano/ Biondetti Alfa Romeo over the gallant Tazio Nuvolari, who challenged throughout in his Cisitalia despite being a very sick man. Maggi decided to compete as a late entry with his old friend Marchese 'Tonino' Brivio in a Fiat 1100 cc sports car and they performed magnificently. Despite being in acute pain and still weak from a major stomach operation, Maggi, then forty-three, shared the driving with Brivio, finishing thirteenth overall. His biggest regret was that his boyhood friend Mazzotti, one of the 'four musketeers' was not there to greet him. An Italian air force pilot, Mazzotti had been reported missing in a war-time flight over the Mediterranean and was never heard of again. The 1947 Mille Miglia was Maggi's last race.

5 TWO PRESIDENTS SHOW HOW IN 1947

'In our sport, they don't mint men like Maggi any more. He was a leader and the inspiration and the golden thread who wove the Mille Miglia into the history books.'

ENZO FERRARI

Although World War II, which devastated Europe, had ended in 1945 it was to take conte Aymo Maggi another two years of determined struggle to get his beloved Mille Miglia back on the battle-scarred roads in 1947. But despite his efforts it was no more than a national event and did not gain international status. Relations between the Automobile Club of Brescia and overseas connections had barely reopened and there was still an element of antagonism and suspicion towards Italy.

The 1947 event, the first to be held on a round-Italy road circuit since 1938 – it had been banned in 1939 and run on a closed triangular circuit in 1940 – was originally scheduled for 27 April. But in order to give the Fiat factory in Turin more time to produce a new 1100 cc model in sufficient quantity, the running of the fourteenth Mille Miglia was delayed until 21–22 June. As many of the bridges over the river Po had been completely destroyed and the customary north-east route back to Brescia from Piacenza was still impassible, it was necessary to incorporate a long, rectangular detour to make up the distance. This went west from Piacenza through Asti to Turin and then turned east, via Novara, Milan and Bergamo to the finish at Brescia along

Conte Aymo Maggi had many friends throughout motor racing and the automobile industry. He is seen here, right, with Tazio Nuvolari

150 miles of autostrada. The name Mille Miglia was really a misnomer, for competitors actually had to drive 1,823km, or 1,139 miles over a hazardous route. The difficulties in getting the Italian rail, road and transport systems operating efficiently again were immense so the same route was used in 1948. To this day the citizens of Turin, home of the Italian motor industry, and Milan, the country's commercial centre, feel affronted that the classic event passed their way only twice in thirty years.

In the preceding years Italy had been under German occupation, heavily bombed by the allied airforces, and fought for every inch of the way from Reggio di Calabria to the Austro-Swiss border: in 1947 it was both a physical and a political mess. The people were tired and depressed and when news of the 1947 edition of the Mille Miglia was announced, it was like a beacon blazing in a pitch-black sky. It represented the chance for every sporting Italian to throw off the shackles of depression, dust down his trusty saloon car, which had been hidden in a barn for the past eight years, and get behind the wheel again. Mille Miglia magic was in the air, but there were two major problems to overcome. Petrol, which had been virtually

CONTE MAGGI'S MILLE MIGLIA

Tazio Nuvolari, left, with his mechanic Scapinelli in a Ferrari before the start of the fifteenth Mille Miglia in May 1948 (*Neil Eason-Gibson*)

impossible to obtain, was still rationed and motor car tyres a black market commodity. It was only due to the persistence of Maggi and Renzo Castagneto that special concessions were made by the fuel companies and Pirelli tyres to make a full tank of petrol and five new tyres available for every competing car. It was like Manna from Heaven and the number of original

entrants rose to the unheard-of level of 245 cars. Obviously, these concessions had to be made in the days immediately before the race and so they were dispensed at the official scrutineering. Sad to relate, wartime deprivations proved too much for ninety of the original entrants, who never had any intention of starting the race: they just drove back to their homes with a full tank

and a new set of tyres, infuriating the petrol companies and depriving Pirelli of 450 of its precious stock.

Maggi made his own contribution to the legendary 1947 event, for about a week before the start he made a last minute entry for his old friend, marchese Antonio 'Tonino' Brivio and himself. Although still only forty-four, Maggi was not now a fit man, and only a short time

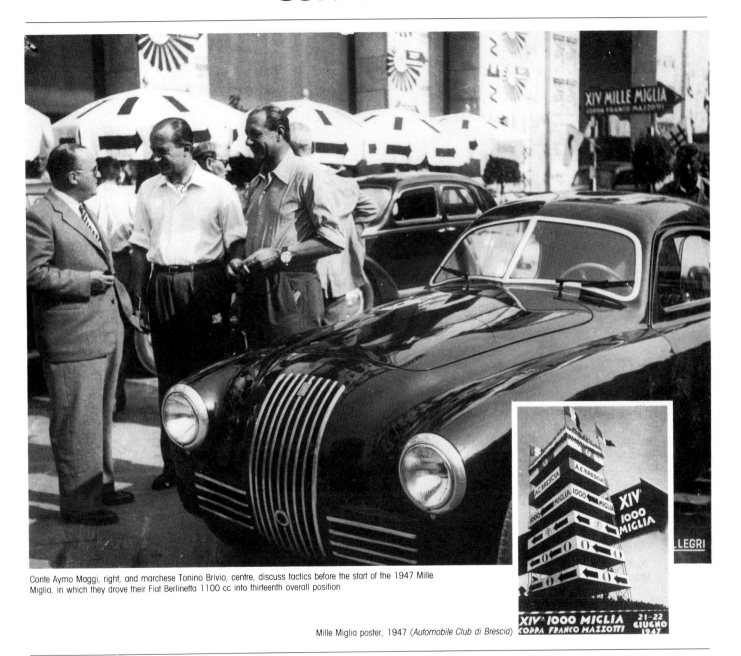

Conte Aymo Maggi, right, and marchese Tonino Brivio, centre, discuss tactics before the start of the 1947 Mille Miglia, in which they drove their Fiat Berlinetta 1100 cc into thirteenth overall position

Mille Miglia poster, 1947 (*Automobile Club di Brescia*)

CONTE MAGGI'S MILLE MIGLIA

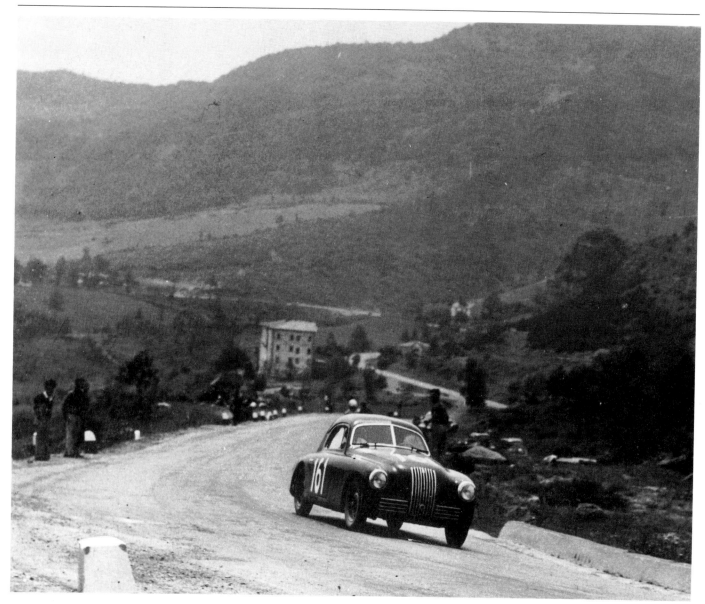

The Fiat saloon of conte Aymo Maggi and marchese Tonino Brivio en route to their magnificent thirteenth place overall in the 1947 Mille Miglia, after lying fifth. They lost valuable time after damaging the sump on a wartime pontoon bridge

before the race he had undergone major stomach surgery. However, he was determined to drive in what was to be his last motor race as a competitor, in a career which had lasted twenty-six years. As he completed his entry he told Castagneto, 'At least I'll know the way as I plotted the route, so that will help us a bit.'

Maggi and Brivio had obtained one of the new factory-prepared Fiat 1100 cc 'Berlinetta' sports saloons, which were fast and aerodynamically functional. At the start they looked like a pair of English country squires, with their light blue sweaters and Harris tweed jackets. There were sixty cars entered in the 1100 cc sports class, of which there were fifty Fiats and five of the exciting new lightweight Cisitalias. These were made in Turin by the talented driver and designer, Piero Dusio, with former Fiat engineers Dante Giacosa and Giovanni Savonuzzi, and incorporated modified Fiat parts.

Both Maggi and Brivio had impressive records in grands prix and sports car events and could be rated with such giants as Antonio Ascari, conte Brilli Peri, Rudi Caracciola, Guiseppe Campari, Louis Chiron, Tazio Nuvolari, Bernd Rosemeyer and Achille Varzi. Maggi had won the Rome grand prix, the circuit of lake Garda twice and the Coppa Etna, while Brivio had had many successes with OM, Bugatti and Alfa Romeo. He had won the Targa Florio in 1933 and 1935, the Tripoli grand prix in 1937 and had driven superbly in grands prix at Monaco, the Nurburgring and Monza. Second overall in the 1932 Mille Miglia with conte Didi Trossi, he won it outright with Ongaro in the Alfa Romeo in 1936. His winning time then was 13 hours 7 minutes 51 seconds and he drove the last 50 miles back to Brescia in the dark without lights, beating the Farina/Meaza

Conte Aymo Maggi, left, and Tazio Nuvolari at the fifteenth Mille Miglia in 1948, both men showing the strain of illness

92

The fond memory, the sheer physical presence of Aymo Maggi is always with us and can never be forgotten. I cannot believe he is not still beside me, this man who since he was a youngster dedicated his whole life to sport.

I think of Aymo as a boy much younger than me. He was always interested in hunting and often went shooting with his friends, particularly in his older days. One recalls his motor-cycling days on the small track at Brescia stadium, giving his rivals a lesson with his brilliant riding and beating them easily. From motor-bikes his switch to four wheels was smooth and after getting experience with a Fiat sports saloon, he moved to Bugatti, the legendary vehicle of its time, and soon became a very real contender. He was brilliant in 1925 and 1926, winning the Rome grand prix and lake Garda twice. In 1927, going for his hat-trick at Garda, he was leading Nuvolari on the last lap when a burst tyre cost him victory.

For a time Aymo was fascinated by flying, and under the instruction of his lifelong friend Franco Mazzotti, successfully completed his private pilot's course at Cinisello. But he didn't pursue this early passion, and it was obvious to me that his true love was cars.

Maggi was always restless, always doing something different and was never still for a moment. It seemed he had to stir the waters of the pool constantly and look for a new reflection to appear – some idea, some

Renzo Castagneto, left, who master-minded every one of the Mille Miglias, with conte Aymo Maggi

exciting scheme or new project. His attitude to life was dynamic and his grasp of technical problems immediate.

Soon after the end of World War II, Maggi tried to get the race going again with his old friend, Bruno Boni, mayor of Brescia. Together they laid down a preliminary plan, but from the outset we faced enormous problems, with the communications network wrecked and many rivers spanned only by shaky temporary bridges. Roads were pot-holed and broken and there were reports of mines left behind on roads by the retreating German army. We worked out a provisional route by trial and error, Maggi driving whole

sections to see if they were possible. He worked and argued with politicians and leading civic authorities all over Italy, constantly nagging and bullying them into action – and he never gave up.

I am quite certain that without the Mille Miglia the entire Italian roadbuilding and reconstruction programme after the war would have been delayed for years. It became a question of national pride and after that first successful post-war Mille Miglia on 21 June 1947 the authorities realised what a powerful public relations weapon the Mille Miglia was in bringing Italy back into the limelight after its disastrous war. But although Maggi was pleased with the race's post-war debut, he was disappointed with the lack of foreign entries. He was well aware that the Le Mans 24-hour race always attracted a strong overseas field and at his insistence I organised a meeting with senior officials there. This visit became an annual pilgrimage and before long Maggi's charm and personality had persuaded several French manufacturers to take part in our race. With Charles Faroux, doyen of the French automotive press, Maggi instituted a major trophy, the Le Mans-Mille Miglia Cup, to be awarded to the driver with the best aggregate position from both races each year, and this was fiercely contested.

Such was the high regard for Maggi in France that in June 1955, the year of the horrific accident in which the French driver

RENZO CASTAGNETO

A perfect shot of the scrutineering in the piazza Vittoria, Brescia before the fifteenth Mille Miglia in 1948

A poster issued for the sixteenth Mille Miglia in 1949, with an inset of race director Renzo Castagneto

A giant birthday cake made for the Automobile Club di Brescia to celebrate the fifteenth running of the Mille Miglia in 1948

Pierre Levegh and eighty-one spectators were killed, he was the official starter of the Le Mans race at the invitation of the Automobile Club de l'Ouest, an honour traditionally given only to motor sports' leading figures. The annual pre-race publicity for the Mille Miglia at Le Mans resulted in a big increase in foreign drivers between 1952 and 1955.

I also remember those gala evenings Maggi created in Paris at which trophies won by the French drivers at Brescia were presented before a celebrity audience and the French press, led of course by Charles Faroux. And our own receptions in the Teatro Grande in Brescia when the Italian drivers received their awards, when Maggi not only offered his congratulations, but also his thanks for their

taking part. The Mille Miglia became known as the best motor race in the world and for this Maggi was truly grateful.

Then there was that tragic accident in 1957, after which the race was banned completely. Maggi, for whom the Mille Miglia represented a way of life and the ideal which determined his every action, would not consider any change in the make-up of the race, which had become a household word. When it was suggested in 1958 that the Mille Miglia should be run in a different guise, he felt it would be a hollow sham of his great race and refused to have anything more to do with it. With the death of the nobleman of Calino in 1961 the world lost a real sportsman who, since the early days of motoring, had maintained his

enthusiasm and beliefs, a tough, controversial figure who clung to his cherished principles through thick and thin. Without him, motor sport could never be the same. I miss him as a friend, a real friend with whom I spent the best years of my life – and mourn his passing. But I don't consider Aymo dead: he is always near, a gem of wisdom and advice.

CONTE MAGGI'S MILLE MIGLIA

Clemente Biondetti awaits the start of the 1948 Mille Miglia in his Ferrari 166S V12 1995 cc with co-driver Giuseppe Navone. Conte Aymo Maggi kneels beside the car, and Renzo Castagneto, left, his hands behind his back, wearing his traditional grey trilby, is also in attendance. Biondetti's switch from Alfa Romeo brought him his third victory (*Neil Eason-Gibson*)

Alfa Romeo by just 32 seconds. Both Maggi and Brivio were also top motor sport officials, Maggi being president of the Associazione Sportiva Automobilistica Italiana and Brivio president of the Commissione Sportiva Automobilistica Italiana, the Commission Sportive Internationale's Italian branch.

Not surprisingly, some of the younger drivers, who had not even been born when the first Mille Miglia was held in 1927, could not understand why the number 161 Maggi/Brivio Fiat 1100 cc was waved off the starting ramp with such enthusiasm by Castagneto, who had despatched and welcomed back every car since those pioneer days twenty-one years before. With the roar of

the crowd in their ears, Maggi and Brivio sped east to Verona and Vicenza and into the Padua control in fifth place, ahead of Tazio Nuvolari's Cisitalia and only two seconds behind the leader; then south, through Ravenna and Rimini to Pesaro on the Adriatic, lying seventh. After crossing the rugged Apennines, having now gone 446 miles, they reached Rome in 6 hours 48 minutes, and lay fifth. Then they headed north along the west coast route through Civitavecchia to Leghorn – which the last of the American forces of occupation had left only six months before.

They were in sixth place overall at Leghorn and on the 72 mile section to Florence in torrential rain when disaster struck. As they crossed a precarious wartime pontoon-bridge across a river, the sump of the Fiat grounded heavily on the uneven surface and oil started to leak as the car slewed to a halt. They managed to repair the damage temporarily and eventually reached the Florence control in 2 hours 17 minutes, compared to the leading Guiseppe Gilera Fiat, which had been 80 minutes faster on that section.

Tazio Nuvolari, race winner in 1930 and 1933, was having an agonizing drive in the open sports Cisitalia. Constantly short of breath because of exhaust-damaged lungs from his many previous races, and coughing blood, he was forced to drive with his head outside his car in order to breathe in fresh air. Such was his distress that he dropped to eleventh place, but recovered to finish in second place after a truly heroic drive.

The accident before Florence was a severe blow for Maggi/Brivio and gave them the sixty-ninth fastest time for the section and dropped them down to nineteenth overall. Undeterred, the two weary champions sped on over the Futa and Raticosa passes to Bologna. After heading north-west through Modena and Piacenza to Asti, they drove superbly on the 35 mile run to Turin and were sixth fastest, just 33 seconds separating the next four Fiats.

Maggi and Brivio recovered the final 150 miles down the autostrada from Turin to Brescia in just under 114 minutes to finish thirteenth overall out of fifty-four finishers in 18 hours 44 minutes 4 seconds, some 62 minutes ahead of their nearest rival. The race was won by the Alfa Romeo of Emilio Romano and Clemente Biondetti (who had won it in 1938 with Stefani and was to win again in 1948 and 1949) in 16 hours 16 minutes and was the last of the eleven race victories by the famous Alfa Romeo marque. Ugo Stella had founded Alfa in 1909 as the Anonima Lombardo Fabbrica Automobile, but the first cars bearing the Alfa name did not appear until 1910 when the last Darracqs had been assembled in the Milan factory. An Italian industrialist, Nicola Romeo, bought the factory in 1915 and the first Alfa Romeos were marketed in 1919.

Wreathed in smiles, Maggie and Brivio linked arms and walked away from the car to rapturous applause. But as they left the finishing-line Maggi turned and said to the waiting Castagneto, 'Renzo, we've got to do something about getting more foreign entries next year. You and I had better go to the Le Mans 24-hour in June and tell them about our race,' . . . which they did together for the next ten years.

6 RACE HAZARDS

'To me, the Mille Miglia was certainly the finest road race of them all, but although I loved it, I was always afraid of taking part.'

STIRLING MOSS

One of the major problems facing drivers of the Mille Miglia was getting used to the millions of race fans, or *tifosi*, as they were called. This descriptive Italian word, used in medical circles to denote the jerky, uncontrollable spasms of those suffering from diseases of the nervous system, in Mille Miglia terminology depicted those completely unpredictable enthusiasts who seemed oblivious to danger and spelled trouble for unwary drivers. The fans lined the route every inch of the way – 10 million was a conservative figure – men, women, children, dogs and even babies standing in the road to watch the approaching cars. Often it was impossible to see the way ahead and the *tifosi* only jumped clear at the very last moment, 'playing chicken' Italian-style.

Most British drivers who competed more than once invariably commented on how much quicker they were able to drive on second, or subsequent attempts. They became hardened to aiming the car straight into a solid wedge of people, knowing, or hoping they knew, that miraculously the road would clear for them to scrape past the outstretched arms and legs; whereas on their Mille Miglia debut they found themselves

Tommy Wisdom, British racing driver and journalist, had a fine Mille Miglia record. He is seen here at the start of the 1951 race (Jaguar). Race director Renzo Castagneto stands, left, next to conte Aymo Maggi with Basil Cardew, motoring correspondent of the *Daily Express*, fourth left (*Neil Eason-Gibson*)

tapping the brakes constantly to avoid what looked like certain disaster.

Some Italian drivers, who had a more naturally flamboyant style, had their own form of shock treatment for the more troublesome fans. They entered corners at very high speed, braked hard, changed down into the appropriate gear and flicked the steering wheel from side to side, causing the rear of the car to fish-tail violently. This invariably cleared the corner quickly as the crowd really thought the car was out of control, and the driver was able to accelerate away, his speed unabated. Effective but tiring tactics over a complete 1,000 mile circuit.

Another technique was used by conte Gastone Brilli Peri, who died while practising in a Sunbeam of the Scuderia Materassi for the Tripoli grand prix in 1930. One of Italy's toughest and most audacious drivers, he had already won the 1925 Italian grand prix at Monza and was leading the 1927 Mille Miglia at Rome when he had to retire his Alfa Romeo with a broken oil-line. He finished fifth in 1928, but retired again in 1929 when lying fourth overall. In each of those Mille Miglias he wore a silver whistle round his neck on a strong lanyard: he cleared the route by blowing long whistle blasts as he approached the corners, hoping to frighten spectators into a standing high-jump to the safety of the pavements.

In the 1955 Mille Migla, when I was still assistant racing manager of the Aston Martin team, all three works Aston Martins failed to finish and so it was a disastrous race for us. I was in charge of our depot at Pescara that year and as two of the three cars had been abandoned in my sector, I had to take a mechanic to recover them and return them to Casa

The author, left, and Peter Collins return to Calino, Brescia after the 1955 Mille Miglia in which Collins' Aston Martin retired near Senigallia with engine failure. Collins was killed when his Ferrari crashed in the 1958 German grand prix at Nürburgring (*Avon Tyre Company*)

Maggi at Calino where we were staying. Peter Collins, who had been driving alone in the open Aston Martin DB3S, had survived a bad accident when the off-side rear tyre burst at high speed between Monselice and Rovigo. A piece of rubber tread weighing about twelve pounds had hit the side of his blue helmet, leaving an angry black mark, and the car had spun wildly down the middle of the road and come to rest between two large trees. Collins had then taken fifteen minutes to cut away the damaged bodywork, but had got going again and made up time rapidly on his run south to Senigallia on the Adriatic coast. But then there had been an expensive bang and the motor had seized solid, ending his race dramatically. When the roads opened again someone had given him a lift back to Fano where I met him in the local bar surrounded by a bevy of girls listening to his stories with delight. That year the Aston Martin team had been running on Avon tyres and when the tyre pressure on his car had been checked afterwards by one of its technicians, it was found to be only 27 psi. This appeared to be too low for the harsh race conditions and it seemed that

CONTE MAGGI'S MILLE MIGLIA

Ron Flockhart in the 1957 Mille Miglia (Jaguar) (*Giannino Marzotto*)

Avon was being optimistic, especially as other competitors were using 45–57 psi.

On our way back to Calino, Collins and I stopped to look at the scene of another accident which the Scottish driver Ron Flockhart had survived in his Austin-Healey during the early stages of the race. Flockhart had approached a right-hand corner, flanked on either side by a stone bridge with a low parapet, at speed. As he had been sliding through the bend an Italian boy had thrown a ball of tightly-rolled newspaper into the road from the kerb on his left and Flockhart had swerved instinctively to the right. The car had smashed violently through the parapet and had overturned in mid-air.

A small river ran under the bridge, which was about fifteen feet above it, and a thick tangle of grass and reeds grew on either side. Flockhart had been thrown clear and had landed on the muddy bank without injury, apart from a bump on the head, and the Austin-Healey had come to rest on the riverbed, clouds of steam pouring from it and all four wheels spinning. Within seconds the whole area had been alive with *tifosi*, who had rushed down the gentle slope to help, several jumping into the water up to their waists. Frantically they had lifted the car, fearing that the driver was trapped beneath and had already drowned. But Flockhart had soon recovered his senses and had run down the bank to the car, only to be completely ignored by the crowd, who

were pushing and shoving and arguing heatedly about the best way to tackle the salvage operation. By the time the car had been righted, everyone was soaking wet and covered with mud – but a groan had gone up when they had seen the driver was not there. For a moment they had looked non-plussed, but then they had run off as though they had seen a ghost; for they had seen Flockhart looking round to claim his belongings and covered from head to foot in thick black mud.

Pat Griffith had joined the Aston Martin team in 1952 and in the 1954 Mille Miglia had been a passenger with Peter Collins in the open DB3S, when they had experienced their own race hazard:

We left Brescia at an unearthly hour. Somewhere between Ravenna and Pescara Peter went fast into a left-hander, but instead of straightening up on the exit, we continued to drift out to the right and hit a kilometre stone hidden in the grass verge. Although the rear of the car on Pete's side looked a little bent, there seemed to be no permanent damage, so I changed the wheel while he smoked a cigarette and calmly enjoyed the scenery. Our minor excursion didn't seem to worry Collins at all and we really pressed on after Pescara to Rome and Viterbo and by then we had forgotten the incident. We were climbing the Radicofani pass before Siena, when suddenly the right rear tyre burst and we shot straight over the edge on my side. We slithered down the mountainside and came to rest against a small tree fifty or sixty feet below the road. By then I had jumped over to Collins' side and was sitting on his lap. As the car teetered on the edge of a sickening drop, Peter said, 'Pat, I never knew you cared!'

Luckily a whole crowd of peasants rushed down and helped us manhandle the Aston back up onto the road, where we changed the damaged wheel. The tyre had obviously been out of alignment since we had hit the kilometre stone and had been rubbing against the body. We set off again, our enthusiasm somewhat dampened, and made it to the Florence control about fifty miles further north and after inspection we were withdrawn on team orders. Collins was a little narked and convinced we could have got back to Brescia, but when the Aston Martin mechanics jacked up the rear, we saw that things were not right. Although Alberto Ascari was well in the lead and went on to win in the Lancia, it was maddening to see Clemente Biondetti, the King of the Mille Miglia, with four victories in 1938, 1947, 1948 and 1949, streak through Florence after us and to learn later that he had finished fourth overall behind Vittorio Marzotto's Ferrari and Musso's Maserati.

Every year the Mille Miglia drew a very wide selection of drivers, ranging from established grands prix and sports car drivers, veteran rally and road racing drivers to quite a few rabbits, who quite frankly were out of their class. In 1955, for example, there was a record entry of 521 cars, and several of the popular Fiat 500 cc category were seen carrying salamis and bottles of Chianti on the back seat and a family photograph on the windscreen.

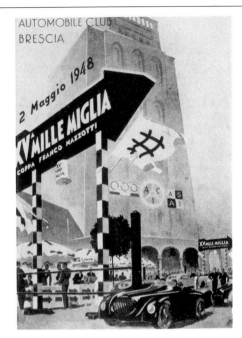

Mille Miglia poster, 1948 (*Automobile Club di Brescia*)

Individual drivers approached the Mille Miglia in entirely different ways, some, like Stirling Moss, completing at least sixteen training laps, or 16,000 miles of competitive driving over open roads for several weeks before the start. Other drivers did not know whether to turn left or right at the end of the viale Rebuffone in Brescia and drove each part of the route as it unfolded before them. An example of this was in the 1955 Mille Miglia, when a Jaguar saloon drove slowly up to the Aston Martin refueling depot at Pescara and stopped by the large transporter. The driver, tall, elegant John Heath, the British joint owner of HWM cars at Walton-on-Thames, wound down the window and said, 'Hello, boys. Can you possibly tell me the way to

Rome?' One of the mechanics replied, 'First right over the bridge, John. You can't miss it!' Heath thanked him profusely, refused a chicken sandwich and went on his lonely way, the car radio playing loudly. He had made no practice laps at all and this really was his first run in the Italian classic. But he died in a tragic accident in the Mille Miglia the following year, when after crashing without apparent injury and being pulled clear, he was laid beside the road to await help. He struggled to sit up and died when a broken rib pierced his heart.

On 13 April 1930, Tazio Nuvolari, the 'mantovani volante' or the 'flying Mantuan', had a fine victory in the Mille Miglia (he won again in 1933) with co-driver Battista Guidotti, when their Alfa Romeo broke the 100 km (64 mph) barrier for the first time since the race began in 1927. On his triumphant return home to Mantua after the race, he received a telegram from a fan which said, 'After your resounding victory, my wife and I plan to give our new son your name and he will be christened Tazio Rino Salvador.' Celebrating his win and toasting the baby, Nuvolari told friends that he felt driving in the Mille Miglia was like drinking an exotic cocktail: 'You might not be able to name all of the ingredients, but once you have sampled it, you could never forget the taste.'

Now in his eighties and a wine grower from Colombaro di Cortefranca, near Brescia, Giacomo Ragnoli was one of the Mille Miglia's true gentleman drivers. He competed fourteen times, starting in 1932. He was always an amateur driver and was founder of Brescia's *Scuderia Mirabella* and took part whenever possible just for the fun of it. Ragnoli takes great pride in the fact that he was

100 ▷

Enzo Ferrari had a long association with the Mille Miglia between 1927 and 1957: first as a driver – he was ninth overall in 1930 with Giulio Foresti in an Alfa Romeo; then as race director of the highly professional and successful Alfa Romeo team, entered as Scuderia Ferrari, and finally as patron of Ferrari cars.

The first two cars to be built by Ferrari as an independent constructor appeared in the wartime Brescia–Cremona–Mantua–Brescia circuit race on 28 April 1940 – officially the '1st Gran Premio Brescia della Mille Miglia' cup, but known as the thirteenth Mille Miglia – under the guise of 'Vettura 815'. As Ferrari's agreement with Alfa Romeo precluded him from using his own name, these 1.5-litre, straight 8-cylinder '815' sports cars, largely comprising Fiat components, had been made under the name of Auto Avio Costruzioni. They were driven by Alberto Ascari (who was world champion in 1952 and 1953 and winner of the

Commendatore Enzo Ferrari speaks at a Club Mille Miglia reception, listened to attentively by conte Aymo Maggi, right

1954 Mille Miglia) partnered by Minozzi (the famous Alfa Romeo driver of the 1920s and one-time riding mechanic with Antonio Ascari and the marquis Lotari Machiavelli di Modena), with Enrico Nardi, a close friend of Ferrari and designer of the ND car with Danese, as co-driver. The two Ferrari prototypes had an unhappy outing and both retired, but only after leading their class and showing real potential. Ferrari cars had a phenomenal record in the Mille Miglia in later years, winning eight of the eleven post-war races held.

How can we possibly truly remember this sportivo Bresciano, this unique sportsman? He was a wonderful example to us all, as a proud nobleman of purpose and as a driver of repute. But, more than that, he was a leader and the inspiration and the golden thread who weaved the Mille Miglia into the history books.

My memory of motor racing goes back to September 1908 when my father took my older brother and me to watch the Coppa Florio race on the Bologna circuit. I was fascinated by the sight and sound of those mighty machines and watched in awe as Felice Nazzaro won in his Fiat at 73.5 mph. I went home in ecstasy, covered in spray from the passing cars, and could hardly wait until the next year when I saw the Record del Miglio at Modena. There were no asphalt surfaces then and it took place over a flying mile on the dirt road near Navicello, between

Commendatore Enzo Ferrari briefs Carlo Pintacuda on the opposition at the Imola control during the 1935 race. Pintacuda and Della Stuffa were the eventual winners (*Ferrari Archives*)

Modena and Ferrara. I actually stood next to such giants of the day as Carminati, Ceirano, Da Zara, Gioia and Scipioni. The Record del Miglio called for the cars to be at top speed as they crossed the start line and Da Zara covered the mile in just over 41 seconds at a speed of 88 mph. From that moment I knew my life would never be the same, motor racing would be my destiny.

My first real chance came when Ugo Sivocci gave me a job at the small CMN factory and he was beside me when I made my racing debut in my own CMN car on 5 October 1919 at Parma in the Parma-Pioggio de Bercetto hillclimb. Apart from the car I had no funds – nothing in my pocket and even less in the bank – but I was full of hope and determination. It was wonderful, I finished fourth in the 3000 cc class and knew the applause of the crowd for the very first time.

Later that year, I took part in my first real road race on the Targa Florio in Sicily. I left

COMMENDATORE ENZO FERRARI

Milan and drove down to Naples with Sivocci to get the ferry to Palermo. We were crossing the Abruzzi mountains when we ran into a snow-drift and were attacked by a pack of wolves, but they ran off when I fired a revolver at them. I eventually finished ninth in the race, which was won by André Boillot's Peugeot, but I was saddened to learn that his car had killed a spectator who ran out into the road from behind a section which was only roped off. In 1920 I drove an Isotta Fraschini and a 4.5-litre Alfa Romeo, with which I came second overall in the Targa Florio, and in 1921 I began my long association with Alfa Romeo as an official team driver and later director, finishing second to Guiseppe Campari in the Coppa Mugello in Florence. In 1923, the year that he won the Targa Florio in his Alfa Romeo, Sivocci was killed while practising for the Italian grand prix at Monza. I was heart-broken, for he had been my constant guide and mentor in my formative years as a driver.

I had a wonderful year in 1924 with Alfa Romeo, winning the circuit of Savio at Ravenna, the circuit of Polesini at Rovego and the Coppa Acerbo at Pescara with Eugenio Siena, Campari's cousin. I feel that my victory at Pescara and the one at Alessandria in 1928, were two of the best races of my career, which by then centred on running the Scuderia Ferrari team of Alfa Romeos, which had such an impact on many pre-war Mille Miglias, winning ten out of the twelve races.

I first met conte Aymo Maggi in the pioneering days of motor sport in the early 1920s and remember him driving his Bugatti skilfully at Porta Romana in Milan. And I knew him with his faithful mechanic Rino Berardi, who with Maggi's financial help established his own machine-tool shop in Brescia in 1925.

In March 1927 I waved to conte Maggi as

An early shot of conte Aymo Maggi at the wheel, talking to Enzo Ferrari

he climbed the Raticosa pass between Bologna and Florence, when he drove in his own Mille Miglia in the massive 8-cylinder Isotta Fraschini with Bindo Maserati, senior test-driver of the Milan-based firm.

That spring of 1927, motor sport where I lived in Modena was in a turmoil. Our local club had since its inception wanted to become like a national body and so we decided to run a major event, the first organised by the club. It had held a few sprints and races before, but nothing much, one on the via Emilia, two trials on the famous 'mile' run outside town and a five-lap regularity race. So, obviously, we wanted the meeting to be a success and get lots of publicity and bring ourselves to the attention of the ruling body in Milan. When the entries started to come in, I was delighted to see Maggi's name among them, for he had already won the Rome grand prix, the circuit of lake Garda twice, and he was one of the best drivers in Europe. Our newspapers gave the event a good review; such was the fame and popularity of the man.

The Brescian pair Minoia/Morandi won in the Brescia-built OM, but Maggi had a worthy drive in the Isotta to finish sixth overall in just over twenty-two hours at an average of 43 mph. Out of the seventy-seven starters from

Brescia, fifty-four completed the 1,000 miles, although the Lavergne/Laubergue Peugeot which came third in the 750 cc class took 37 hours 50 minutes 33 seconds to make the round trip.

Two months later, on 5 June, Maggi came to Modena for the first Modena grand prix, which I won with the new 1500 cc 6-cylinder Alfa Romeo, ahead of Attilio Marinoni (Alfa Romeo). Maggi drove his Isotta Fraschini in the over-3000 cc class, in which there were the Italas of Emilio Materassi/Micatti and Damiano Rogai/Carlo Pintacuda, who went on to win the Mille Miglia in 1935 and 1937. Maggi set a new lap record on the fifth lap, but had to retire on the following lap.

In our sport they don't mint men today like Maggi any more. He was someone on whom you could always rely. A warm, sincere person who whatever the situation or the problem, expressed himself with clarity, frankness and unbiased good humour. In 1957, when the Mille Miglia was banned after de Portago's death and the race was sought to be re-introduced as a timed regularity trial, Maggi bowed out. It was no longer his race, his Mille Miglia, that splendid and inimitable event which Maggi, Mazzotti, Castagneto and Canenstrini created and proved to all the world.

CONTE MAGGI'S MILLE MIGLIA

In the 1948 Mille Miglia Tazio Nuvolari lost his bonnet cover and damaged the front left wing which pointed upwards. Without stopping Nuvolari shouted, 'Hold tight!' to his mechanic and drove against the side of the bridge to knock the wing off completely, but failed to finish the race (*Ferrari Archives*)

actually classified as a finisher in eight of the fourteen races, an honour shared only by Tazio Nuvolari and Cabianca. In fact only eight other drivers had a better finishing record than Ragnoli: Franco Cortese (14), conte Cornaggio Medici (15), Archimede Rosa (12), Adolfo Facchetti (11), F. Apruzzi, Clemente Biondetti, Ovidio Capelli and conte Giovanni Lurani (9 each).

Like all Mille Miglia veterans, Ragnoli is full of anecdotes and his favourite concerns his 1932 debut when he drove a Fiat 514 MM. He and his co-driver were heading south from Bologna on the road to Florence and climbing the Futa pass, when their car shot off the road on a difficult bend. There was a parked ambulance standing nearby, but both Ragnoli and his passenger were unhurt, and walked unaided into the local hostelry on the corner and downed several brandies each to settle their nerves.

The following year, Ragnoli approached the same corner with particular caution, just noticing the same ambulance out of the corner of his eye. But in that split second his concentration wavered and he crashed once more in the identical spot. Both drivers were again unhurt and walked back to the same bar, where the owner was nonchalantly polishing glasses. When he looked up he exclaimed, 'What, you two again! Did you notice we moved the ambulance nearer the scene of the accident this year, so that you would have less distance to walk if you had been injured!'

On another occasion, Ragnoli's Fiat boiled its radiator dry on a hilly section and came to a halt with steam pouring out. Leaving his passenger to do what he could, Ragnoli started to run up the hill

Giacomo Ragnoli is presented with a special trophy by conte Aymo Maggi at the lunch given for Brescian drivers following the nineteenth Mille Miglia in 1952. Ragnoli, a true 'gentleman' of the Mille Miglia, competed in the race fourteen times and finished in eight (*Giacomo Ragnoli*)

towards a group of fans standing on a bank, shouting '*acqua, acqua*', 'water, water'). Pretending that he thought Ragnoli was a competitor in the round-Italy cycle race which had passed through the previous weekend, one of the *tifosi* poured a bucket of cold water over Ragnoli's head in the same way as he had done to the racing cyclists – but it was some time before the radiator cooled and they were able to creep into the next control.

In some ways, the race organisers were lenient in their interpretation of the regulations. It has been suggested that a

special category was sometimes introduced to ensure that a particular car of unusual specification might have a chance of winning its class. There were, however, two points on which the organisers were adamant: a competing car could have one or two drivers (one only from 1954), but a third person was never to be carried, not even in a saloon car; and, *most importantly*, no substitution of driver or passenger could take place once the competitor had left the via Rebuffone in Brescia – the same crew had to start and finish, or they would be disqualified summarily.

But tensions ran high in the Mille Miglia

Piero Taruffi drove in fifteen Mille Miglias before winning the last in 1957. He is seen here, at the wheel, with Mario Vandelli in 1952, but their Ferrari 4100 cc V12 340 America retired with mechanical trouble (*Neil Eason-Gibson*)

CONTE MAGGI'S MILLE MIGLIA

This photograph, taken at one of the controls on the 1950 Mille Miglia, captures the whole essence of the race. The Osca 1100 sports car, driven by Luigi Fagioli, with Diotallevi left, has stopped short of the control and is being waved on by the Automobile Club official. The co-driver clutches the route card ready for stamping, watched by thousands of spectators. Note the skid marks and the potentially hazardous tramlines leading through the town. They finished seventh overall and won their class in 14 hours 34 minutes 44 seconds (*Neil Eason-Gibson*)

In 1950 Jaguar entered a strong team in the Mille Miglia for the first time: Biondetti/Bronzoni, Leslie Johnson/Lea, Tommy Wisdom/Hume and Haines/Haller. Seen here at the start of the race are Johnson/Lea who brought their Jaguar XK 120 home in fifth place overall (*Neil Eason-Gibson*)

and in the 1937 race Casalis, an Italian driver from Piedmont, drove a Fiat Siata in the 750 cc sports car class with his co-driver Marone. They crashed badly on the Futa pass and although Casalis was unhurt, Marone was badly injured and had to be rushed to hospital by ambulance. Casalis worked frantically on the car and having got it going after emergency repairs, noticed another race car which had broken down nearby, the crew still sitting in it. Casalis coerced one of them into joining him and got back on the road. They motored several hundred miles together and were checked through the Rimini control, but on leaving the city Casalis took the wrong route and headed along the coast towards Ravenna instead of striking inland for Forli and Bologna. After retracing their tracks they rushed into Bologna, where his 'companion of the night' was thrown out by officials and put on a bus back to Florence. A lonely Casalis completed the course to Brescia, only to get a severe reprimand from the race director and disqualification for his pains.

The enthusiasm of the young race fans was tremendous and most of them dreamed of the day when they would be old enough to get a competition licence and take part in the great event themselves. In 1955 two young boys aged twelve and ten, who lived on the route in Verona, decided that they could not wait.

Knowing that the large group of little 500 cc Fiats, the 'topolinos' or 'clockwork mice', would go through Verona in the dark, they borrowed their mother's similar car, painted on false race numbers and infiltrated the race without trouble. Driving at breakneck speed for mile after mile they were really enjoying themselves. But they had made one mistake: they had

CONTE MAGGI'S MILLE MIGLIA

not checked the fuel tank on the car and so they ran out of petrol and their race ended in tears at the side of the road. Race officials who walked over to the parked Fiat were at first furious when they discovered it was not a proper race car, then amazed to find that the occupants were not even teenagers. The boys were mildly rebuked and later driven home.

But conte Aymo Maggi heard about the incident and on the Monday after the race he had the boys collected from their home in Verona and taken to an official luncheon in Brescia to honour the British winners, Stirling Moss and Denis Jenkinson, and seated them between himself and Fangio. The boys had been in tears and frightened when an official had called for them, fearing that they were being taken to prison. They certainly had not expected to be pardoned and fêted at an emotional lunch, and promised that they would be back in the Mille Miglia when they were old enough to take part. Sadly, the race was banned two years later and they never had the chance.

Stirling Moss recalls a worrying incident which happened to him and Denis Jenkinson when they were practising for the same 1955 Mille Miglia with the Mercedes 300SL coupe. They had already completed several training laps – always on open roads, as the Mille Miglia route was never closed except on the actual race weekend – but they were still covering the 1,000 mile circuit in about thirteen hours, despite the bustling traffic. Up to 1938, this would have been a race-winning time.

Although the fans appreciated and even encouraged their flat-out training speeds, the *caribinieri* in the towns and the *polizia stradale* on the roads did not

share their wild enthusiasm, as Moss remembers:

We were following an army lorry one day outside Forli on the way south to Rimini, when it suddenly changed direction sharply in front of us. I did everything I could to miss it, but we hit the side with a terrible bang. Uproar broke out and we were horrified to learn that the lorry was packed with racks of bombs in the back. Luckily a local motor sport enthusiast stepped out of the crowd who spoke good English. With his help we were able to telephone Alfred Neubauer, the Mercedes team director in Brescia, before being taken to the police headquarters in Forli.

We waited for ages in the basement of the police station, before suddenly being marched down a long stone corridor and we really seemed to be heading for the dungeons. Then our escort told us to stop beside a carved wooden door and we were ushered into the magnificent presence of the Chief of Police, while our temporary interpreter was left outside. The chief was wearing an immaculate grey-blue uniform with gold epaulettes and several rows of decorations, and he sat behind an ornate mahogany desk. 'Now, we're in trouble,' we thought. But without warning and in perfect English, he said, 'What a wonderful race the Mille Miglia is. I drove in it last year in a Stanguellini 750 sports. I didn't win as the car broke down, but at least I had the satisfaction of having taken part. I wish you both the best of luck in this year's race and if there is anything you need at any time

Stirling Moss, right, winner of the 1955 Mille Miglia with Denis Jenkinson, with Bruno Boni, president of the Brescian Chamber of Commerce, before the start of the 1987 Mille Miglia for historic cars. Moss's time of 10 hours 7 minutes 48 seconds was never beaten (*Foto Eden*)

please let me know.'

We were dumbfounded to be free again and to be able to walk back down the corridor and step outside into the fresh air. No wonder we gave the crowds in Forli a big wave as we passed through on our way to victory that year.

Although women drivers were eligible to compete in the Mille Miglia and did so from time to time, they did not have many successes. One of the most spirited drives by a woman was in 1929, when the popular actress Mimi Aylmer entered in a Lancia Lambda. She arrived at the start, wearing a smart red dress and fur jacket and looking cool and immaculate, and with her chauffeur at the wheel. Few of the thousands watching thought that she would drive herself, but at the last moment she took over and the chauffeur was relegated to the passenger seat, where he was to stay throughout the race.

She drove the entire distance herself

Cartolina trasportata dal corridore
BIONDETTI N. 546, partito da Brescia
alle ore **5.46** e arrivato alle ore

One of the postcards carried in the 1953 race by Clemente Biondetti (*Ferrari Archives*)

and arrived at the outskirts of Brescia more than a day after she had left. To the amazement of the race fans she pulled off the road for a five minute break while she attended to her hair and make-up, and having put on fresh lipstick, rejoined the race. She was flagged across the line by Renzo Castagneto just twenty-five hours after the start to the rapturous applause of the crowd, stepping out of the car with a radiant smile, perfectly groomed and with no sign of fatigue. Her chauffeur, however, looked tired and ill and was later given a special award at the prize-giving, for being the most 'courageous' man of the race. Seventy-two cars had started and forty-two returned, Mimi

Aylmer making twenty-ninth place overall after an Oscar-worthy drive.

Renzo Castagneto, race director of the Mille Miglia from its inception in 1927 until the race was banned after the 1957 event, was well known for his talent in public relations and his sense of theatre, which he used to such good effect over the years. In the 1953 race a mail bag, containing a selection of printed postcards, was carried in the Lancia driven by Clemente Biondetti. On the front of each postcard, addressed to conte Aymo Maggi at the Automobile Club in Brescia, was a drawing of the Brescian driver Nando Minoia, stating that he had won the first Mille Miglia in 1927 with Morandi in an OM car. The reverse was headed with the legend '20th 1000 MIGLIA' and said that the postcard had been carried by the driver Biondetti whose race number was 546 and that he had left Brescia at 5.46 in the morning and arrived back at . . . – with a gap for the finishing time. The postcards were collected from the finishing line and rushed to the main post office, where the arrival time was inserted and they were then delivered to the Automobile Club before breakfast on the morning after the race, so that Maggi could send them to philatelists all over the world. Biondetti had a good drive that year, finishing eighth overall in just under 11 hours 50 minutes, so his precious cargo could still be franked at 5.36 in the evening of the race and yet had travelled 1,000 miles during the day.

Tazio Nuvolari won the 1930 Mille Miglia with co-driver Gianbattista Guidotti one of the most famous Alfa Romeo test-drivers, and they were partners again in

1932 in one of the several Scuderia Ferrari Alfa Romeos entered by Enzo Ferrari. As they approached the Florence control, near the piazzale Michelangelo, Nuvolari made an uncustomary mistake when his attention wandered for a fraction as he spotted that his team-mates Pietro Ghersi and Guilio Ramponi (winner in 1928 and 1929) had gone off the road and he too lost control. Ghersi and Ramponi were only slightly injured, but the car was too badly damaged to continue.

As Nuvolari's Alfa Romeo headed for, and finally crashed into a tree, a frightened Guidotti jumped over the side, somersaulted onto the road and was knocked unconscious – crash helmets were not compulsory and were rarely worn then. When he came round, there was no sign of Nuvolari and Guidotti found himself on a stretcher, flanked by four sinister figures, wearing long, flowing cloaks with hoods over their heads, and eyes shining through two slits. Still weak and confused, he thought he was being led away to some secret ceremony by the Klu Klux Klan, so he closed his eyes and pretended to be dead. In fact his stretcher-bearers were devoted brothers of the strict Confratelli della Misericordia from Florence, who since medieval times had helped the needy and who were taking him to the hospital at the monastery for treatment – a service they had voluntarily provided for the injured for every Mille Miglia.

Further down the road, near Ancona, the Alfa Romeo of the great champion Giuseppe Campari was also in trouble. Campari, who had won in 1928 and 1929 (both times with Ramponi), had finished third in 1930 and second the previous year, loved to sing as he drove and wanted to be an opera singer, but he was also fiercely competitive. He was

CONTE MAGGI'S MILLE MIGLIA

Clemente Biondetti was one of the Mille Miglia's most successful drivers, winning the race four times. Here he climbs the famous cobbled *Scale di Piantonia* between Parma and Il Poggio de Berceto in his open 2000 cc Ferrari in 1949 (*Millanta*)

well-placed in the 1932 race when he handed over for a breather to his mechanic Sozzi, who promptly crashed the car into a wall and put them out of the running. Sozzi was heart-broken and in tears after the accident, but he soon pulled himself together again as the burly Campari chased him down the road brandishing a hammer from the tool kit.

In the 1955 Mille Miglia I was in charge of the Aston Martin pit at Pescara during the race and Captain George Eyston, racing director of Castrol ran our second depot at Siena. We were all staying at Casa Maggi near Calino and while the team was kept busy on its training programme, Captain Eyston and I left Brescia in the Lagonda station wagon to make a final check on the refuelling arrangements with Esso in Pescara and Siena, set up during an earlier visit. Eyston, tall and bespectacled, had been on the racing scene for many years and was well known as a racing driver and as three-times holder of the world land speed record in the 36.5-litre twin-engined Thunderbolt. At his last attempt in 1938 he had averaged 357 mph over the mile at Bonneville in America. He was a direct descendant of Thomas à Becket and his vitality and energy were boundless.

On Saturday, 23 April at about 6.30 p.m. we were just south of Florence when there was an expensive-sounding noise from the rear axle, and when we crawled underneath, we saw the casing was glowing red. With the axle whining in protest, we crept slowly down the road and found a small garage. When the garage owner saw the 'IN PROVA 1000 MIGLIA' (on Mille Miglia practice) sticker on the vehicle it was like a magic password: within seconds the Lagonda

Drama in the 1951 Mille Miglia with the Ferrari 340 America of Gigi Villoresi, the famous F1 driver, and co-driver Cassani. They went off the road at Ravenna, severely damaging the left front wheel and suspension and had to cut away the body to change the wheel. Heavy rain slowed them further, but cleared at Bologna, and Villoresi won by 20 minutes from Giovanni Bracco. In several of the Mille Miglias the weather was terrible, making the race extremely difficult, especially for drivers of open sports cars who were often soaked to the skin for fourteen or fifteen hours (*Ferrari Archives*)

was over the inspection pit and shortly afterwards the mechanic reported that all the bolts had loosened and the axle was completely drained. The only remedy was to motor into Florence and find a replacement – in the wet at 9 p.m. on a Saturday night. As Eyston had an urgent pre-race commitment in Brescia before the start the following weekend, I stayed in Florence to try to repair the car. I had heard that the Lagonda axle was identical to that on a Jeep and the next morning the hotel porter gave me the address of a large Fiat garage in town, and I drove round in the fast-expiring Lagonda to see if I could get it fixed.

I was met by two tired-eyed

mechanics who had worked all night on a long-distance coach, but when I said I had to return to Brescia immediately because of the Mille Miglia, their inborn love of motor racing sprang to the surface. Despite their lack of sleep, within a short space of time the damaged axle had been stripped, cleaned off in petrol and the broken gears laid out neatly for inspection. One of them had a friend who ran a parts depot and after a heated telephone call in which 'Mille Miglia' was mentioned several times, he arranged for the store to be opened, even though it was Sunday morning. We rushed round, and outside found the proprietor who let us into a long

CONTE MAGGI'S MILLE MIGLIA

After a suberb win in the 1950 Mille Miglia with Marco Crosara, Giannino Marzotto became known as 'the man in the double-breasted blue suit'. He emerged from his winning Ferrari 195S Berlinetta Le Mans after a thirteen-and-a-half hour drive looking immaculate in a suit made from material woven at the Marzotto family's textile mills. At twenty-two, Giannino Marzotto was the youngest ever Mille Miglia winner (*Neil Eason-Gibson*)

warehouse with rows of neatly stacked shelves.

Having checked the parts catalogue to confirm to me that the serial numbers on the Lagonda gears were identical, the owner went to the appropriate rack. There I was amazed to see hundreds of Jeep rear-axle units in sealed cartons, no doubt 'borrowed' at the end of the war ten years previously. The carton he selected was boldly stamped 'US FORCES IN ITALY' and the whole assembly was wrapped in a protective coating of waxed oil-cloth, thick with grease.

Before long, back at the garage, the replacement axle had been carefully reassembled and the car was ready for road testing. They had then worked twenty-nine hours without stop, first on the Fiat bus and then on the Lagonda, and yet they were prepared to strip the axle down and start again if requested. The total cost for the job, including labour, parts and a large tip was £22.

I left Florence immediately and headed north for Brescia, thirty-six hours behind schedule. The Lagonda was going like a bomb, and even better than

before, since the new axle ratio was slightly lower than the old and gave the car tremendous acceleration out of corners. It was an amusing drive back that Sunday afternoon, as not only was I on the Mille Miglia route, but also on the course for the Taranto-Milan motor-cycle race. I found myself running half an hour ahead of the race-leaders, and thanks to the 'IN PROVA 1000 MIGLIA' windscreen sticker on the car I was waved on by every policeman and cheered the whole way by the crowds lining the route.

7 CONTE MAGGI AND THE BERARDIS

'The Mille Miglia was an event which not only provided enormous technical advances, but it really did breed champions.'

ENZO FERRARI

The association between conte Aymo Maggi and Rino Berardi was a long and happy one, dating from the mid-1920s until Berardi's death in 1948. It resulted in motor racing successes together, in the design and construction of aircraft and marine engines and two Maggi-Berardi racing cars, which have seemingly disappeared from the face of the earth, and it resulted in the foundation of the Officine Meccaniche Berardi in Brescia, which celebrated sixty years of technological evolution in 1986 and is now a world leader in the manufacture of automated production systems.

Aymo Maggi began his racing career in 1922 with a Chiribiri and later switched to Bugatti, scoring numerous successes with the elegant cars designed by Ettore Bugatti and built in a disused dye works at Molsheim, Alsace. The 'patron', as Bugatti was called, was an extrovert character, Italian by birth, German by nationalisation and living in France, and a noted bon viveur and bloodstook fancier.

By 1925 Maggi was one of Europe's leading drivers, having won the Rome grand prix and the circuit of lake Garda (which he won again in 1926) and was a frequent visitor to Molsheim, becoming close friends with Bugatti and sharing his

Rino Berardi, at the wheel of the first Maggi-Berardi car in 1925 (*Aymo Berardi*)

Mille Miglia poster, 1950 (*Automobile Club di Brescia*)

time between there and Milan. During one such visit Bugatti suggested that Maggi should open an agency for Bugatti cars, and promised him an exclusive franchise for all racing and touring cars for the whole of Italy. Knowing that Bugatti was the first manufacturer to sell grands prix cars commercially and that he would always be offered the latest racing machinery for himself, Maggi readily agreed and opened a Bugatti showroom and service department in Porta Roma, Milan.

It was directly through the Bugatti agency that Maggi and Berardi began their partnership which was to thrive for more than twenty-three years. Born in Brescia, Berardi was a mechanic who longed to make his way in motor racing and in 1925 when he was nineteen his chance came when Maggi

Conte Aymo Maggi, left, and Rino Berardi with the Berardi-Maggi two-stroke air-cooled radial aircraft engine they designed (*Aymo Berardi*)

Conte Aymo Maggi and Rino Berardi were well-known figures on motor racing circuits all over Europe. They are seen here after another victory in their Bugatti at the circuit of lake Garda in 1926 (*Aymo Berardi*)

gave him a job in Milan. A skilled engineer and technician, Berardi worked happily on the preparation of Maggi's racing cars and those of wealthy clients and often went with him to Molsheim to collect cars from the factory. He was also a sensitive test-driver, or *collaudatori*, so impressing Bugatti that he was often invited to stop on at the factory to test the latest models and report his findings; high praise indeed from a man accepted to be 'a trained artist first, a

mechanical genius second and an engineer last of all'.

In the early days of racing there was often a close association between the established driver and his travelling mechanic, who was probably a factory test-driver and spent much of his life behind the wheel. Such an unbreakable link, enhanced by the risks they shared, was formed between Maggi and Berardi, who became his co-driver, mechanic and constant companion. They won

races all over Europe, and used the publicity from these victories to boost sales from the Bugatti agency.

As a result of his friendship with Berardi and his personal faith in him, in 1926 Maggi decided to give him financial backing to establish his own engineering shop in via Ferramola, Brescia. There, using overhead drilling machines of his own design, Berardi took in specialised metalwork for finishing. The business made gradual but steady progress with the help of Rino's wife Maria and his brother Aldo and the support of several of Italy's leading automobile manufacturers, such as Alfa Romeo, Fiat and Isotta Fraschini, who came to him with more complex requests for their own particular needs. The factory then started to design and construct new machine tools for many different industries and eventually, after World War II, to supply entire fully-automated systems of the highest technical standards. Today, Berardi's son Aymo, the present chairman, who proudly bears the christian name of his father's benefactor, is head of a multi-national organisation supplying production systems and technical research programmes in the aerospace, automotive, oil, robotic and thermo-nuclear industries.

While the Berardi company was establishing its engineering reputation, Maggi and Berardi were still maintaining a heavy motor racing schedule, and they found time to design and construct two of their own Maggi-Berardi, or MB single-seater racing cars. The first of these, in 1925, was a front-wheel drive car with a 1500 cc 4-cylinder engine, aluminium body and disc wheels, which was built partly in one of Berardi's workshops and partly at the Maggis' town house in via Musei, Brescia – where neighbours frequently complained about the noise of racing engines being stressed to breaking point in the small hours of the morning.

The second Maggi-Berardi single-seater was built in 1926, with rear-wheel drive, a 1500 cc 4-cylinder engine mounted ahead of the driver, slab-sided aluminium body, brass radiator and disc wheels. Both cars carried a round enamel badge on the radiator with the initials MB, where the right-hand upright of the letter M forms the downstroke of

The second Maggi-Berardi car built in Brescia in 1926, conte Aymo Maggi at the wheel and Rino Berardi, right (*Aymo Berardi*)

Conte Aymo Maggi at the wheel of the second Maggi-Berardi car built in 1926. Conte Franco Mazzotti stands behind, left, and Rino Berardi, right (*Aymo Berardi*)

Conte Aymo Maggi at the wheel of the second Maggi-Berardi, Rino Berardi behind him (*Aymo Berardi*)

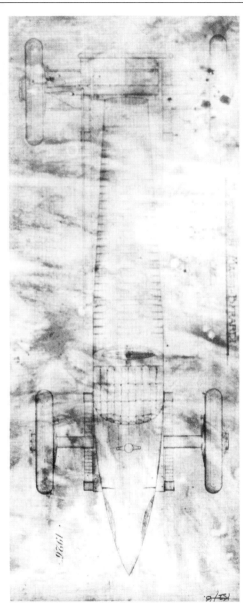

A plan of the rear wheel drive Maggi-Berardi, 1926 (*Aymo Berardi*)

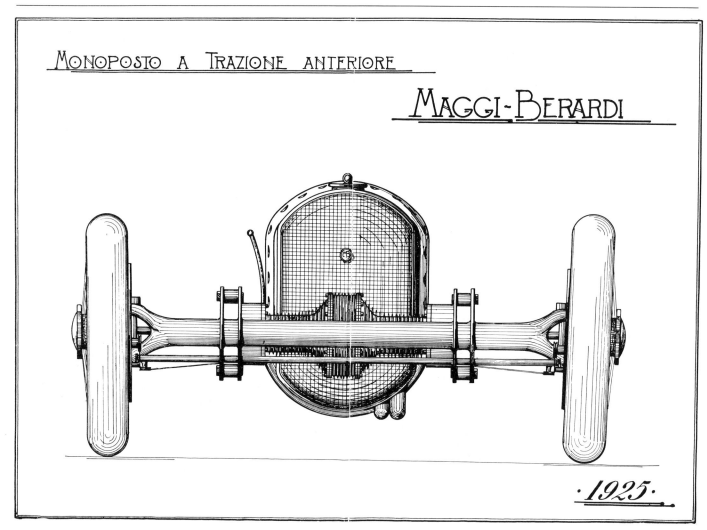

MONOPOSTO A TRAZIONE ANTERIORE

MAGGI-BERARDI

·1925·

Plan of the revolutionary front wheel drive Maggi-Berardi built in 1925 *(Aymo Berardi)*

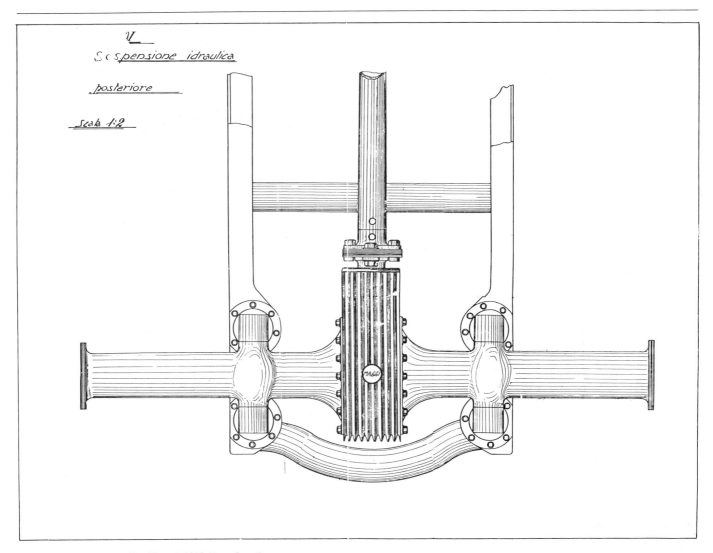

The rear hydraulic suspension Maggi-Berardi, 1926 (*Aymo Berardi*)

It was seven o'clock in the evening on Sunday 2 May 1954, when my good friend Elia Filippini and I crossed the finishing line in the viale Rebuffone, Brescia. The streets were almost deserted, the chairs and spectator stands were being packed away and the banners brought down, as we returned from the Mille Miglia, one of the last to finish from the original field of 374 cars, in 167th position.

We were exhausted. We had been battered by cyclonic winds and torrential rain and had driven through thick fog in the early part of the race. But, nevertheless, we had managed to complete the course in our first attempt, at the wheel of our Fiat 1100 Berlinetta. It was an emotional moment, for ever since I was a schoolboy and had helped out with the scrutineering in the piazza della Vittoria, I had sworn that one day I would drive in the big race.

The winner, Alberto Ascari in his Lancia 3300 had covered the 1,000 miles in 11 hours 26 minutes at over 87 mph. We had left the ramp shortly after midnight and had taken 19 hours 10 minutes 24 seconds. I knew that our small moment of motor racing history was nothing really but, even so, as finishers we would now be entitled to wear the coveted red-arrow lapel badge, or distintivo bearing the words '1000 MIGLIA', and we had thereby qualified to join an élite club. Then, as we sat in the car relaxing for a moment, conte Aymo Maggi, who as usual had waited for the last stragglers to return, walked briskly over. He was wearing his typical English-look grey trousers and turn-ups, checked jacket and brown hat, and carried a tightly-furled black and white chequered flag. Leaning down from his impressive height, he tapped on the roof of the car and said in his gruff Brescian voice, 'Bravo Vigliani, bravo Filippini. Next time get rid of your inhibitions and stop staring at the wall.' I was bone-weary, nauseous from petrol and exhaust fumes and my eyes danced from having had the windscreen wipers sweeping across my vision for the last nineteen hours, but at the same time I was elated at having finished.

The following year, on 2 May 1955, I returned to the fantasy world of the Mille Miglia with a different friend, Giancarlo Sala, and in a faster car. We left Brescia in our Alfa Romeo 1900 TI at 3.44 a.m. on Sunday and got back in 13 hours 14 minutes 57 seconds to finish second in the over 1300 cc class. That year was the fantastic victory of Stirling Moss and his red-bearded passenger, Denis Jenkinson, a brilliant technical journalist and former triple world champion sidecar passenger, in their silver Mercedes in 10 hours 7 minutes 48 seconds. No one would ever beat his time in that hectic, poetic race.

The great Italian ace Tazio Nuvolari had died in August 1953 and in his honour Maggi had introduced in 1954 a special 'Gran Premio Tazio Nuvolari' — a prize for the fastest time recorded by any driver on a timed section on the ultra-fast home run of

Stirling Moss, centre, after the 1955 victory, with team-mate Denis Jenkinson, left, and conte Aymo Maggi

the 'three cities', Cremona–Mantua–Brescia. Mantua, of course, was Nuvolari's birthplace, so you can imagine the crowds who turned out to cheer on their idols. In 1955 Stirling Moss won the award in 39 minutes 54 seconds and the last Mille Miglia of all in 1957 was won by Piero Taruffi's Ferrari, but he was some twenty minutes slower than Moss who thus retained the honour of being fastest-ever on the full 1,000 miles. But the glory of winning the Tazio Nuvolari trophy at the fastest speed came in 1957, when the Belgians Olivier Gendebien and Philip Washer finished third overall in their Ferrari 3000 GT. They covered the Cremona–Mantua–Brescia section in 39 minutes 43 seconds, an average speed of 124.6 mph. Think what it meant to drive at such speeds on ordinary Italian roads, even if they were closed to traffic, and realise some of the anguish it caused in built-up areas with residents of towns and villages.

MANUEL VIGLIANI

Conte Aymo Maggi, who always 'looked like an English gentleman'

Conte Aymo Maggi, centre, with his Bugatti, and travelling mechanic, Rino Berardi, right. Conte Berardo Maggi, Aymo's father, stands behind the car (*Aymo Berardi*)

the letter B, confirming its designation as a Maggi-Berardi car.

Later in 1926, Maggi, Berardi and conte Franco Mazzotti built a third single-seater racing car, which was designed as a formula 'Junior' car, and which was claimed at the time to be the world's smallest monoposto car. This unique car was front-engined and called the

Maggi-Mazzotti, or MM, and for several years the red-painted little machine was left hanging tail-down from a bracket on the garage wall at Mazzotti's palazzo at Chiari. It was later removed to a motor museum in Turin.

That the two Maggi-Berardis were actually built — and were not just design projects — is indisputable. It is also almost

certain that neither of them was ever raced, or driven in any of the numerous hillclimb events, such as the Nave-San Eusebio which took place around Brescia, always a pioneer as a centre of Lombardian motor sporting activities. But what is a complete mystery is the whereabouts of either car, or the fate that befell them. In January 1988, Aymo

In 1952 Giovanni Bracco in the Ferrari Berlinetta drove past the portals of this outstanding fourteenth-century palazzo in Vicenza in the early stages of the 1,000 mile race. Note the dangerously wet roads and the close proximity of the crowds, protected only by a wooden barrier (*Publifoto*)

The Maggi-Mazzotti single-seater `Junior' car designed by conte Aymo Maggi, conte Franco Mazzotti and Rino Berardi in 1926

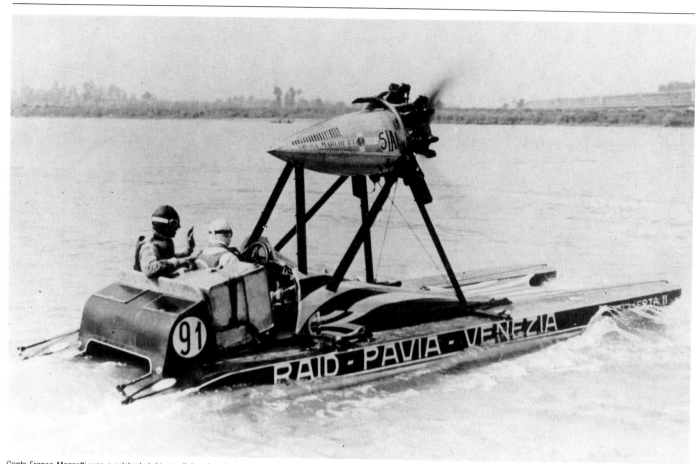

Conte Franco Mazzotti was a celebrated driver, pilot and motor boat champion. He is seen here testing Feltrinelli's hydrofoil on the Venice lagoon. He later built his own boat fitted with a Berardi-Maggi aero engine, with which he won the gruelling Raid–Pavia–Venezia river marathon *(Aymo Berardi)*

Berardi was shown a photograph of the single-seater car with Maggi at the wheel and Rino Berardi looking on and said that this was the *second*, rear-wheel drive Maggi-Berardi and not the front-wheel drive car Maggi and Berardi had built the previous year. Berardi said no-one knew what happened to the cars after 1926, but he then produced

the original machine drawing showing the front-wheel drive Maggi-Berardi, dated 1925. This drawing and a handful of blueprints from other projects was all that had been salvaged from the ruins of the Berardi factory which had been completely destroyed by the RAF in 1944.

Both Maggi and Berardi were meticulous engineers and it seems

incredible that their two hand-crafted racing cars, built with such patience and devotion, should have been mislaid, or even lost completely. Possibly the cars were pushed away into a lock-up garage and are still hidden under a Brescian dustsheet or, as has been suggested, smuggled to the French château home of an American collector.

and Berardi had fiercely-competitive backgrounds and the management was adaptable and always looking for new ideas and markets. With Maggi's continued financial help they designed and produced a successful Berardi-Maggi radial aero-engine in 1930, and later that year a powerful Berardi-Maggi marine engine was introduced, and about fifty were eventually made. But, despite the prospect of substantial sales to the Fascist government, Berardi, for political reasons, refused to go into full production and no more marine engines were assembled.

Motor racing ace Tazio Nuvolari, above, who died in 1953 and his arch rival, champion racing driver Achille Varzi, below, put the *Asso* and the *Aliante*, with their experimental Berardi-Maggi engines, through tests on lake Garda

In the 1930s, speedboat racing, or *motonautica*, was very popular on the Italian lakes and the mirror-like waters of the Venice lagoon and it produced many champions: men like Guido Cattaneo, Pompeo Dolci, Eugenio Silvani, Picci Ruspoli, Aldo Dacco, Maurizio Vasseur, Arnaldo Castiglioni, Mario Speluzzi, Antonio Passarin, Guilio Foresti and conte Theo Rossi di Montelera, president of the Club Gabriele D'Annunzio at Gardone.

Di Montelera had driven an Alfa Romeo saloon in the 1933 Mille Miglia, his noble identity disguised under the pseudonym of 'vecchio tordo', 'the old thrush', and it was he in 1935 who decided to stage an exciting match-race on lake Garda between the two great motor racing champions and rivals, Tazio Nuvolari and Achille Varzi, with boats powered by Beradi-Maggi marine engines. Conte Franco Mazzotti was also an experienced speedboat pilot and with his friends Maggi, Berardi and Guido Cattaneo, built a special hydrofoil which he called *Mille Miglia* and with which he won the famous river marathon, the Raid—Pavia—Venezia, using a Berardi-Maggi marine engine.

It is possible that they might have been lost under the rubble of the bombing raid, but even if that were true, that still leaves an eighteen year gap unaccounted for between 1926 and 1944. At present there is no trace of them, and there has been none for more than sixty years. Yet there must surely be someone who could open this 'Pandora's box' and expose the true fate of these two historic cars.

Between 1926 and 1931, the Berardi company progressed steadily and began making its own machine-tools, capable of machining racing, aircraft and motor-boat engines. This in turn led to orders for other high-technology tools in widely-diverse industries. This early success and growth was largely the result of the company's founding: both Maggi

THE FINAL LAP

'In motor racing, the one who goes the fastest must win. He who gets rid of his inhibitions will always beat the one who lifts his foot. Motor sport is like that. The Mille Miglia has always been like that and will never change. Can you imagine a Mille Miglia being other than a race of speed?'

CONTE AYMO MAGGI

During his illustrious racing career, conte Aymo Maggi drove many cars – Alfa Romeo, Bugatti, Chiribiri (built by Deo Chiribiri), Fiat, Isotta Fraschini, Maggi-Berardi, Maggi-Mazzotti, Maserati and OM. His personal maxim of 'He who gets there fastest wins' never wavered, and it was always his intention that the Mille Miglia should be a speed event. But in the post-war years speeds increased dramatically and not everyone in Italy was happy at the thought of racing cars being driven through crowded streets at speeds of up to 200 mph, and even higher with some grand touring cars, when the public often stood ten-deep on the pavements alongside.

When Maggi heard about the terrible accident at Guidizzolo on 13 May 1957, in which the Spanish nobleman, the marchese Alfonso Cabeza de Vaca 'Fon' de Portago, his American co-driver, Ed Nelson, and ten spectators were killed after their Ferrari burst a left front tyre at high speed and somersaulted down the road, he was heart-broken – for he knew that the race had been run for the last time.

In one way Maggi had already known that it could not go on for ever because of mounting criticism in Italy about the very high speeds that had been

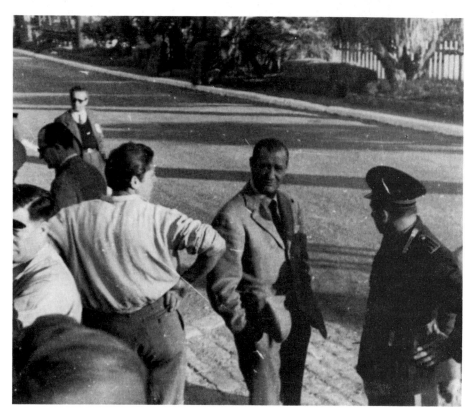

Conte Aymo Maggi in front of the pits at an early post-war race at Ospedaletti, Imperia in 1948

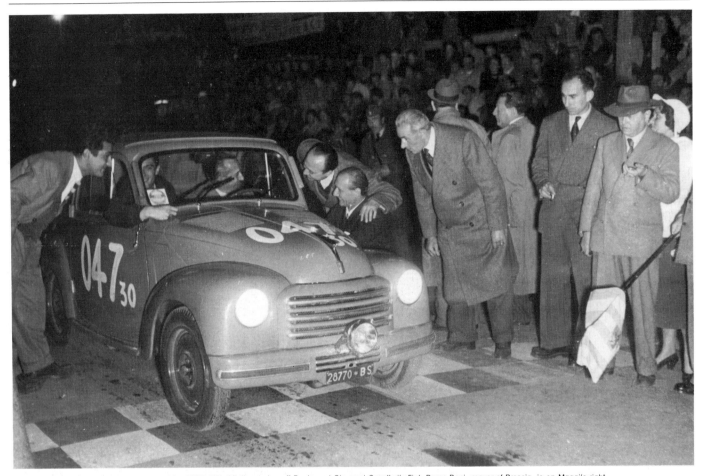

Conte Aymo Maggi, kneeling, at the start of the 1951 Mille Miglia, seeing off Paolo and Giovanni Cavalleri's Fiat. Bruno Boni, mayor of Brescia, is on Maggi's right

achieved since 1953. But he had always hoped that when it did finish, then it would be on a high note and not on a tragic one. Sadly it was not to be. Three days after the fatal accident the Italian government announced the race's ban. Road racing on public roads in Italy had finished.

Enzo Ferrari himself had been waiting at the Bologna control, the last before Cremona on the run back to Brescia, during that final race, and his four works Ferraris were in the first four places. In his view, the situation at Bologna was that Piero Taruffi was leading without problems and being covered by the

German, Wolfgang Trips, with de Portago in an unassailable third position. The Belgian Olivier Gendebien was fourth, driving the new 250 GT Berlinetta sensibly, as it was essential for the export order book for this car to finish well placed.

In his own book, *pilote, che gente*, Ferrari says he is certain that the

CONTE MAGGI'S MILLE MIGLIA

Conte Aymo Maggi did much to encourage British competitors to take part in the Mille Miglia, particularly in the post-war years. Seen here at Calino, Brescia in 1949 is the Healey team: Donald Healey, left, Geoffrey Healey, right and British journalist, Tommy Wisdom, second right. The Healey saloon, No. 356, left, driven by Wisdom/Healey came tenth and won the Touring Class over 1100 cc. Both the team's cars had 4-cylinder 2.4 litre Riley engines (*Neil Eason-Gibson*)

Englebert tyre made at its Liège, Belgium factory blew-out after de Portago's car had crossed the cat's-eyes in the centre of the road and that it was this that caused the tragedy, and which ended the Mille Miglia so abruptly. But, as the constructor and chief executive of Ferrari cars, he faced criminal charges from the government and condemnation in the media, resulting in protracted legal battles and considerable adverse publicity. Four and a half years later, however, Ferrari was delighted to find that all charges laid against him — or Englebert tyres — had been found groundless and that he and his organisation were completely exonerated.

From the moment of the ban, however, nothing was ever the same for conte Aymo Maggi; he seemed to age rapidly, and his vitality and zest for life were gone. He rarely went to see Renzo Castagneto or his old friends at the Automobile Club in Brescia and reacted angrily when approached about the possibility of introducing a revamped

Conte Carlo Castelbarco, left, who was second in the 1933 Mille Miglia to Tazio Nuvolari, with conte Aymo Maggi, second left, Bruno Boni, second right, and Renzo Castagneto, right, before the prizegiving to French drivers in Paris in 1954

Mille Miglia in 1958, which would involve speed sections with a regularity-run format. Manuel Vigliani recalls:

Aymo Maggi, accomplished driver as he was in all types of events, recognised, together with Castagneto, that the speeds being achieved on the Mille Miglia were reaching the upper limits of safety — and were becoming increasingly difficult to control. But he had always contended that motor racing should be solely a question of speed. He was always saying the same thing.

I well remember that after de Portago and Nelson died in 1957, causing the Mille Miglia to be banned in its old form, there was a proposal put forward to change the format, to quench the flames and make it a reliability event . . . in other words to try to domesticate the tiger. Aymo exploded and said with considerable feeling, 'I will never consider anything different. In motor racing, the one who runs fastest must

137

Piero Taruffi was certain that one day he would win the Mille Miglia and eventually he did, but it was only on his fifteenth attempt that it finally came about.

Born in Rome in 1907, Taruffi trained as an automobile engineer before starting to race motor-cycles as a teenager and winning numerous events. He switched to four wheels in 1930, driving an 8-cylinder Bugatti, and joined Ferrari's prestigious Scuderia Ferrari in 1932. During his 27-year career Taruffi, whose prematurely grey hair earned him the nickname 'the silver fox', drove grands prix and sports cars with equal success. He was that rare combination, a fast and safe driver and also a talented racing engineer. In 1938 he won the Tripoli grand prix in his 1500 cc Maserati and in 1948 the Berne grand prix with the new Cisitalia 1100 cc sports car made in Turin, which he helped to design and develop. He also built his own controversial twin-boom record breaking cars, TARF I and TARF II after the war, and established several records.

In 1951 Taruffi was second to Fangio in the Swiss grand prix and won the gruelling Pan-American road race with Luigi Chinetti (Ferrari) at 88 mph. In 1952 he won the Swiss and Paris grands prix and the Ulster Trophy race at Dundrod. He had another fine drive in the 1953 Pan-American road race (Lancia), finishing second to Juan-Manuel Fangio, and the following year had victories in the Targa

Florio, the circuit of Sicily and the Syracuse grand prix. In 1955 Taruffi again won the circuit of Sicily and was honoured by Mercedes with a drive in the Italian grand prix at Monza, where he finished second to Fangio in a similar car. Many of his successes stemmed from his ability to control any type of car at very high speeds on real road circuits and his amazing stamina.

Taruffi's long history of Mille Miglia competition dated back to 1930, when he finished fortieth overall. He was third with Pellegrini (Alfa Romeo) in 1933 and fifth in 1934 with Giovanni Bertocchi (Maserati), winning the 1100 cc class. In 1938 he again won the 1100 cc class with Carena (Fiat) and was sixteenth overall, but then had to wait nineteen years before he won the last Mille Miglia of all in his Ferrari.

LEFT, Piero Taruffi, winner of the last Mille Miglia in 1957 at his fifteenth attempt, was also a talented automobile designer. He built two revolutionary twin-boom prototypes, TARF I and TARF II, fitted with either a Guzzi or Gilera motor cycle engine of 350 cc or 500 cc (seen here), or a 2000 cc Maserati engine

OPPOSITE, In this historic shot Piero Taruffi in his Ferrari 315S waits for his wife Isabella to flag him away for the 1957 Mille Miglia, which he won, watched by conte Aymo Maggi, left, and Bruno Boni, second left (Neil Eason-Gibson)

PAGE 128, Piero Taruffi – the Silver Fox – drives his Ferrari 315S over the Apennines on the way back to Brescia after his historic victory in the 1957 Mille Miglia. He first entered the event in 1930 (Neil Eason-Gibson)

Conte Maggi's Mille Miglia, in which I drove so often, not only improved motor sport generally, but helped the automotive industry, the component manufacturers and the entire national transport system to develop over the years. It gave people from half of Italy the chance to see the latest cars competing for honours under the most difficult conditions and it gave drivers the opportunity to test their cars to the absolute limit under real race conditions. This was a wonderful thing, especially for an engineer like me.

In 1932, when I made my Mille Miglia debut with Eugenio Siena in the Scuderia Ferrari Alfa Romeo 2300 and did not even finish, the thrill of actually competing in such an event sent adrenalin pumping through me. I was determined that I would win it one day. I suppose I felt like Ernest Hemingway's

PIERO TARUFFI

fisherman in The Old Man and the Sea, *who was obsessed with catching one really big fish and nothing else would do. Every year that I was forced to drop out, I was even more determined to do better next time.*

The enthusiasm of the fans was fantastic and it was the sheer magic of speed which drew them to line the route, night or day. After leaving the starting ramp you drove into a funnel-shaped corridor and you had to go easy on the throttle, but for the rest of the race you could drive as though it was a closed circuit. Normally traffic was carefully controlled, although you often passed bicycles on the road and occasionally a car came the other way. The many very fast sections, followed by stretches over mountain passes, certainly helped produce our future champions. One year, the difference between overall first and second place was just 32 seconds after 1,000 miles, and often a difference of only a few seconds could mean a better overall position, or a coveted class win – which for the smaller cars meant as much as outright victory. This 10/10ths driving, or driving to the limit all the way, needed great courage, endurance and tenacity, and also a mental balance. In my opinion, fast flashy drivers never won the Mille Miglia but fast safe drivers did.

My memories of the Mille Miglia are both good and bad. Good ones before the war, with a third and fifth place overall and those two class wins. Then, after the war, those terrible depressions, which started in 1947 when I drove my new Cisitalia 1100 – it was the Italian equivalent of the French Simca as modified by Amedee Gordini and used the same flat-four Fiat engine. After that it was one long series of retirements, year after year and my wife Isabella was getting increasingly worried about my continuing to race. I promised her and Ferrari himself that I would stop for good the day I won the Mille Miglia.

Well after an eternity it finally happened:

A victory salute from 'the silver fox' Piero Taruffi as he walked away from his winning 1957 race. His first attempt at the Mille Miglia had been in 1930, he had lead the race on five occasions, but only succeeded on his fifteenth. Clapping him on the back is Giovanni Canestrini, one of the race's founders (*Neil Eason-Gibson*)

in 1957 at my fifteenth attempt I won driving solo in the powerful Ferrari 4100. My race number was 535, showing the public I had started at 5.35 a.m., and the draw was certainly lucky for me as it totalled thirteen, my lucky number. Team mates Wolfgang von Trips, the German nobleman, and Peter Collins were 532 and 533 respectively, and when I got to Rome, about half-way, Collins was leading me by some five minutes. On the road between Viterbo and Florence I began to see black skidmarks on many of the corners and I knew that Collins was trying just a bit too hard, so I motored on and kept my head. On the last mountainous section from Florence to Bologna, the transmission started to rumble and I thought I was going to have to retire yet again.

But Ferrari himself was at the Bologna

control, where it was raining hard, and he told me that it was dry twenty miles down the road, and that Collins was also having axle trouble. So I left Bologna less worried and determined to nurse the car home, changing gear carefully and motoring at about 145 mph, instead of the 175 mph the Ferrari was capable of. The axle was definitely getting worse and about sixty miles from the finish I saw a red speck in the rear-view mirror, which gradually grew bigger. After several miles it closed and Taffy von Trips roared past me with a wave. I did a quick calculation and reckoned that as I was three minutes ahead of him on the road, I could still win by that amount if only I could keep him in sight. But he started to pull clear and when we reached the small village of Piadena he had gained about two hundred yards.

I knew that there were three fast curves out of the village, and at the first his brake lights suddenly glowed bright red, went out and then came on again momentarily, and soon I was right behind him. That last sweeping curve at Piadena was my 'moment of truth' for I overtook him on the exit, and then I was certain I had won at last. I crossed the line, just a few feet ahead of von Trips, to the wonderful sight of Renzo Castagneto holding out the chequered flag. My time was 10 hours 30 minutes 48 seconds, the second fastest recorded in all twenty-four Mille Miglias and only beaten by that incredible drive of Stirling Moss in 1955 in 10 hours 7 minutes 48 seconds.

Suddenly I found myself receiving a tumultuous welcome from the crowded tribunes, Isabella leaning down to kiss me and taking off my fly-stained helmet for the last time. And then I was shouting, 'I've won, I've won!' On five previous occasions I had led the race; finally I had reached the end of the rainbow.

To win the Mille Miglia was the proudest moment of my life.

CONTE MAGGI'S MILLE MIGLIA

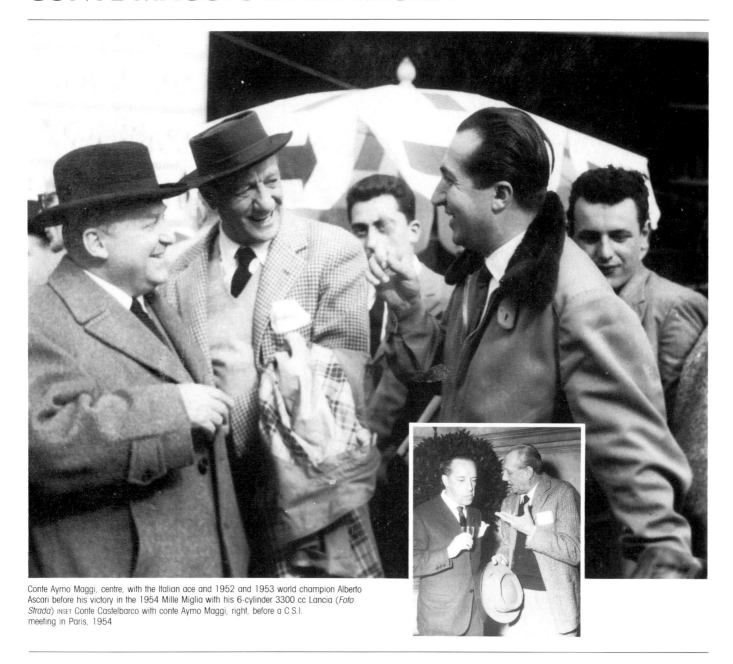

Conte Aymo Maggi, centre, with the Italian ace and 1952 and 1953 world champion Alberto Ascari before his victory in the 1954 Mille Miglia with his 6-cylinder 3300 cc Lancia (*Foto Strada*) INSET Conte Castelbarco with conte Aymo Maggi, right, before a C.S.I. meeting in Paris, 1954

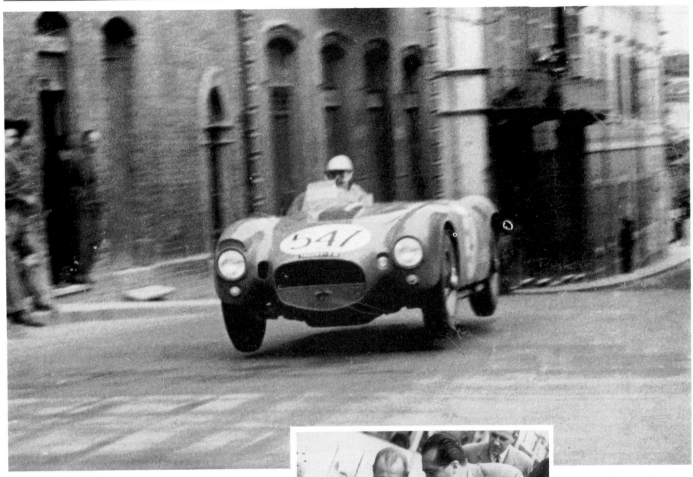

In the 1954 Mille Miglia Lancia entered a strong team of four new 6-cylinder 3300 cc sports cars from Taruffi, Castellotti, Ascari (the eventual winner) and Valenzano. Taruffi led the field at Rome, with 4 minutes advantage on team-mate Ascari, but crashed at Vetralla. He is seen here with all four wheels of the Lancia in the air (*Neil Eason-Gibson*)

Conte Aymo Maggi, seated, with Alberto Ascari, 1952 and 1953 world champion. Ascari was killed while practising at Monza in 1955, just a few days after his Lancia had crashed into Monte Carlo harbour when leading the Monaco grand prix

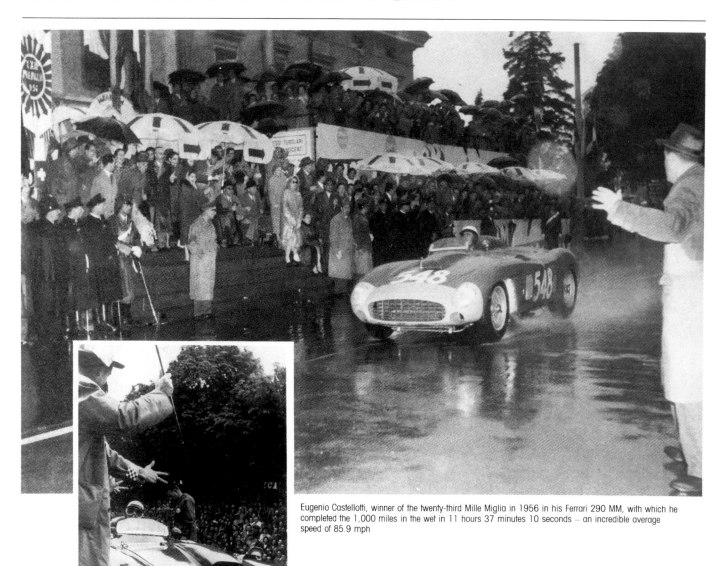

Eugenio Castellotti, winner of the twenty-third Mille Miglia in 1956 in his Ferrari 290 MM, with which he completed the 1,000 miles in the wet in 11 hours 37 minutes 10 seconds — an incredible average speed of 85.9 mph

Eugenio Castellotti, idol of the Italian crowds, who won the 1956 Mille Miglia in pouring rain. Engaged to actress Della Scala and successor to Alberto Ascari as Italian champion, he was killed while testing a Ferrari at Modena in 1957 aged twenty-six (Ferrari Archives)

Bruno Boni, with flag raised, checks the countdown before starting Graf Wolfgang 'Taffy' von Trips, the German nobleman, on his 1,000 mile drive into second place in his open Ferrari 532 in 1957. Conte Aymo Maggi stands behind Boni and Renzo Castagneto is on the right of the group. Von Trips died with thirteen spectators when his Ferrari left the track in the 1961 Italian grand priz at Monza (*Publifoto*)

Fon de Portago and Ed Nelson in the 1957 Mille Miglia before the fatal crash (*Giannino Marzotto*)

Spanish nobleman, marchese Fon de Portago with conte Aymo Maggi before the fatal accident at Guidizzolo in 1957 when his Ferrari crashed into the crowd

After a superb drive Piero Taruffi won the 1957 Mille Miglia in 10 hours 28 minutes in his Ferrari 315S, beating his German team-mate, von Trips, by 3 minutes. Here Renzo Castagneto salutes the victorious Taruffi (*Neil Eason-Gibson*)

A superb picture of the 1957 Mille Miglia. Commendatore Enzo Ferrari, right, tells his team driver, Wolfgang von Trips, that he is lying second to Piero Taruffi, whose Ferrari has rear axle trouble. But Taruffi held off the challenge. This shot shows all the tense action of the final pit stop of a factory team whose cars were about to finish 1st–2nd–3rd, but whose other car, that of Fon de Portago, was about to cause the fateful accident which saw the ban of the Mille Miglia for ever (*Ferrari Archives*)

Mille Miglia poster, 1957 (*Automobile Club di Brescia*)

CONTE MAGGI'S MILLE MIGLIA

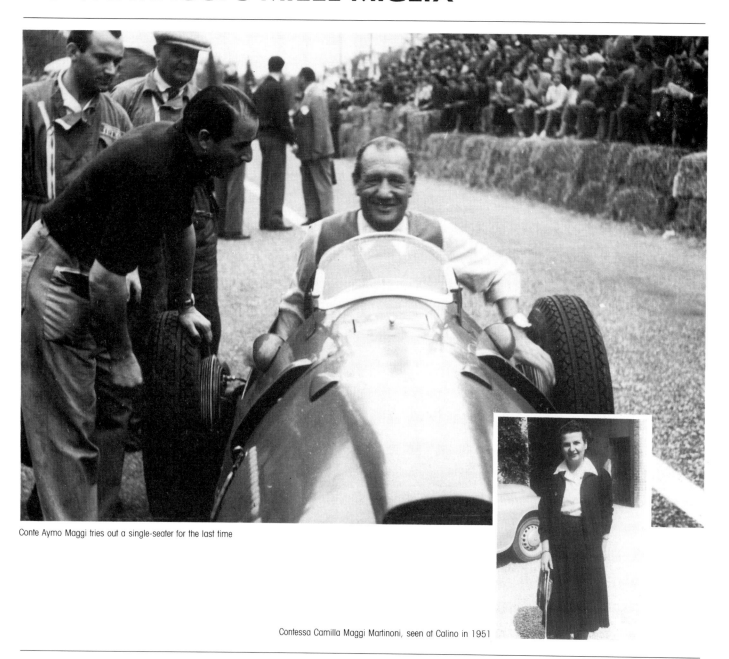

Conte Aymo Maggi tries out a single-seater for the last time

Contessa Camilla Maggi Martinoni, seen at Calino in 1951

Conte Aymo Maggi was an excellent shot and after the banning of the Mille Miglia in 1957 devoted much of his time to hunting

win. He who gets rid of his inhibitions will always beat the one who lifts his foot. Motor sport is like that. The Mille Miglia has always been like that and will never change.'

Then he turned to me and said in a choked voice, full of emotion, 'Dear Vigliani, you've done the Mille Miglia haven't you? You've seen what our race is all about. You're a journalist, don't play the diplomat and don't make compromises. There are too many compromises already in our sport. Tell them the truth, Vigliani. Can you imagine a Mille Miglia being other than a race of speed? If you believe it could, then you do it, because I will not be going.'

How could you not agree with a man like that?

Maggi's hopes of holding on to an old tradition had died. He was no longer a gentleman of motor sport, but a country gentleman who looked after his extensive properties at Calino and Gradella. When

CONTE MAGGI'S MILLE MIGLIA

Giuseppe Morandi, left, with Alessio Brunelli, another driver of the Mille Miglia, towards the end of Morandi's life. First in 1927, Morandi came tenth in 1928, second in 1929 and eleventh in 1947 (*Brunelli Archive*)

Contessa Camilla Maggi presents a special trophy to Giuseppe Morandi at the 1986 Mille Miglia for historic cars. Morandi won the first Mille Miglia in 1927

he visited Brescia from time to time, he would go to see his house at via Musei, occasionally look in to see Renzo Castagneto in his office at the Automobile Club, which overlooked tranquil gardens, and then search through the archives of the old Mille Miglia to recall once again the pungent smell of Castrol 'R', the racing oil with a lingering aroma, from the engine of his beloved Bugattis.

Though still relatively young at fifty-four, he seemed nevertheless to be a man from another age. He could not believe that his cherished Mille Miglia could no longer survive and had gone forever, and although he continued to spend time on his farm at Gradella which he loved, and his vineyards at Calino, his heart was full of remorse. The Mille Miglia, to which he had devoted his life, was over and Italy would never be the same

again. The race which had inspired a nation, and indeed the world, for thirty years was dead, haunted by the ghosts of Guidizzolo.

In 1959 while returning from a trip to the south of France, Maggi suffered a major heart attack. He appeared to recover, but two years later he had a second and fatal attack at Calino, and he died there on 23 October 1961.

POST-RACE

Now, nearly three decades after his death, I often feel the shadow of conte Aymo Maggi beside me, his chequered flag rolled up and beaming his sunny smile. And I remember his wonderful hospitality at Calino with the smiling contessa Camilla always at his side and the warm welcome they offered night or day to the élite from the automotive world.

If the Mille Miglia is not to settle under a cloud of dust and its ghosts laid to rest forever, we must always remember how much we owe to the man who characterised those thirty years of sport: let us all raise our glasses and drink to conte Aymo Maggi – the magician of the Mille Miglia.

MANUEL VIGLIANI

When I talk about the Mille Miglia, I feel quite moved, for it played such a big part in my life. I knew it as a driver, a team director and a constructor . . . and was always an admirer of its champions. In fact, the Mille Miglia not only provided enormous technical advances during its three decades, it really did breed champions.

I was present at every one of the twenty-four Mille Miglias that were run and was numbed by the tragic accident in 1957 when

Conte Aymo Maggi

the marchese de Portago was killed driving one of my cars, causing the race to be banned.

In my opinion, the Mille Miglia was an epoch-making event, which told a wonderful story. The Mille Miglia created our cars and the Italian automobile industry. The Mille Miglia permitted the birth of GT, or grand touring cars, which are now sold all over the world. The Mille Miglia proved that by racing over open roads for 1,000 miles, there were great technical lessons to be learned by the petrol and oil companies and by brake, clutch, transmission, electrical and lighting component manufacturers, fully justifying the old adage that motor racing improves the breed.'

COMMENDATORE ENZO FERRARI

APPENDIX 1
Chronology of the Mille Miglia

1927 Brescia-built OM cars score 1–2–3 victory. A sensational race ensures the Mille Miglia's future.

1928 A strong Bugatti team falls by the wayside. The first victory for Campari/Ramponi's Alfa Romeo.

1929 A second victory for Giuseppe Campari/Guilio Ramponi, with Giuseppi Morandi/ Archimede Rosa's OM not far behind.

1930 Tazio Nuvolari enters the legend with a fantastic win with Gianbattista Guidotti – breaks the 100 kph barrier.

1931 Rudi Caracciola/Sebastian score first foreign win with Mercedes. Campari is second with Marinoni.

1932 Alfa Romeo fights back with Baconin Borzacchini/ Amedeo Bignami first of seven home.

1933 Tazio Nuvolari wins again and Alfa Romeos fill first ten places. British MG team debut.

1934 Fantastic Achille Varzi duel with Tazio Nuvolari lasts the whole race. Varzi wins by eight minutes with Louis Chiron third.

1935 Thinly disguised grand prix cars enter the Mille Miglia. Winner Carlo Pintacuda takes a small passenger.

1936 Wonderful race sees conte Tonino Brivio's Alfa Romeo beat Nino Farina by 12 seconds.

1937 Carlo Pintacuda again. Mussolini's chauffeur finishes fourth and shares team prize with Mussolini's son Vittorio.

1938 Clemente Biondetti wins the last pre-war classic. The race is banned by the Italian government after crowd fatalities at Bologna.

1939 No race. Italian government ban still in force.

1940 'Deutschland Uber Alles' as Baron Huschke von Hanstein's BMW blitzes Brescia circuit.

1947 Clemente Biondetti wins again in first post-war race round Italy after nine years' absence.

1948 Clemente Biondetti's hat-trick sees the first Ferrari victory. Tazio Nuvolari is superb in his last Brescia drive.

1949 A fourth win for Clemente Biondetti sets a Mille Miglia record. A class win for the British Healey.

1950 Giannino Marzotto, the man in the 'double-breasted' blue city suit, wins after an unruffled drive.

1951 Gigi Villoresi wins for Ferrari. Giovanni Bracco is second after a spirited drive in Lancia Aurelia.

1952 Giovanni Bracco wins in Ferrari and foils a Mercedes challenge in a race of 1,000 drivers.

1953 World champion Manuel Fangio's Alfa Romeo dominates the race but final victory goes to Giannino Marzotto for the second time.

1954 A fine win by Alberto Ascari's Lancia over Vittorio Marzotto. Nino Farina crashes out of the race.

1955 Stirling Moss and Denis Jenkinson score a superb victory with Mercedes in record time for 1,000 miles.

1956 Eugenio Castelloti's Ferrari wins in a downpour from Peter Collins, Luigi Musso and Juan-Manuel Fangio.

1957 Piero Taruffi wins at last but Fon de Portago's death brings the Mille Miglia to an end.

APPENDIX 2
Race Winners Classification 1927–57

1ST MILLE MIGLIA : 26–27 MARCH 1927.
STARTERS 77. FINISHERS 54.

1. MINOIA-MORANDI   OM   21h 04m 48s
                         48.27 mph
2. DANIELI T.-BALESTRERO OM   21h 20m 53s
3. DANIELI M.-ROSA   OM   21h 28m 02s
4. STRAZZA-VARALLO   LANCIA LAMBDA   21h 42m 48s
5. PUGNO-BERGIA   LANCIA LAMBDA   21h 55m 14s
6. MAGGI-MASERATI B.   ISOTTA FRASCHINI 22h 00m 35s
7. 'FRATE IGNOTO'-SOZZI   ALFA ROMEO   22h 06m 11s
8. CORTESE-BARONCINI   ITALA   22h 45m 46s
9. GUTTERMANN-MUNARON   ALFA ROMEO   22h 53m 57s
10. NUVOLARI-CAPELLI   BIANCHI   23h 12m 02s

2ND MILLE MIGLIA : 31 MARCH–1 APRIL 1928.
STARTERS 83. FINISHERS 40.

1. CAMPARI-RAMPONI   ALFA ROMEO   19h 14m 05s
                         52.58 mph
2. ROSA-MAZZOTTI   OM   19h 22m 22s
3. STRAZZA-VARALLO   LANCIA   19h 37m 37s
4. MARINONI-GUIDOTTI   ALFA ROMEO   19h 38m 13s
5. BORNIGIA-GUATTA   ALFA ROMEO   19h 42m 00s
6. BRILLI PERI-LUMINI   BUGATTI   19h 45m 44s
7. SCARFIOTTI-LASAGNA   LANCIA   19h 52m 02s
8. PRESENTI-CANAVESI   ALFA ROMEO   20h 10m 55s
9. RADICE-LISSONI   LANCIA   20h 13m 17s
10. MORANDI-COFFANI   OM   20h 26m 04s

3RD MILLE MIGLIA : 13–14 APRIL 1929.
STARTERS 72. FINISHERS 42.

1. CAMPARI-RAMPONI   ALFA ROMEO   18h 04m 25s
                         56.05 mph
2. MORANDI-ROSA   OM   18h 14m 14s
3. VARZI-COLOMBO   ALFA ROMEO   18h 16m 14s
4. STRAZZA-VARALLO   LANCIA   18h 17m 41s
5. GHERSI-GUERRINI   OM   18h 55m 08s
6. MINOIA-MARINONI   ALFA ROMEO   19h 01m 44s
7. NATALI-ZAMPIERI   ALFA ROMEO   19h 04m 37s
8. CARRAROLI-MUNARON   ALFA ROMEO   19h 07m 42s
9. CORTESE-GUATTA   ALFA ROMEO   19h 16m 47s
10. BORNIGIA-PINTACUDA   ALFA ROMEO   19h 17m 17s

4TH MILLE MIGLIA : 16–17 APRIL 1930.
STARTERS 135. FINISHERS 73.

1. NUVOLARI-GUIDOTTI   ALFA ROMEO   16h 18m 59s
                         62.78 mph
2. VARZI-CANAVESI   ALFA ROMEO   16h 29m 51s
3. CAMPARI-MARINONI   ALFA ROMEO   16h 59m 53s
4. GHERSI-CORTESE   ALFA ROMEO   17h 16m 31s
5. BASSI-GAZZABINI   OM   17h 18m 34s
6. CARACCIOLA-WERNER   MERCEDES   17h 20m 17s
7. ROSA-COFFANI   OM   17h 22m 58s
8. MAZZOTTI-MAGGI   ALFA ROMEO   17h 46m 45s
9. FERRARI-FORESTI   ALFA ROMEO   17h 55m 16s
10. FONTANINI-MINOZZI   ALFA ROMEO   17h 57m 14s

CONTE MAGGI'S MILLE MIGLIA

5TH MILLE MIGLIA : 11–12 APRIL 1931.
STARTERS 99. FINISHERS 59.

1.	CARACCIOLA-SEBASTIAN	MERCEDES 63.21 mph	16h 10m 10s
2.	CAMPARI-MARINONI	ALFA ROMEO	16h 21m 17s
3.	MORANDI-ROSA	OM	16h 28m 35s
4.	KLINGER-SACCOMANNI	ALFA ROMEO	17h 07m 57s
5.	FRATELLI GERARDI	ALFA ROMEO	17h 08m 06s
6.	SCARFIOTTI-BUCCI	ALFA ROMEO	17h 27m 36s
7.	TADINI-SIENA	ALFA ROMEO	17h 39m 50s
8.	GAZZABINI-GUATTA	ALFA ROMEO	17h 47m 08s
9.	NUVOLARI-GUIDOTTI	ALFA ROMEO	17h 48m 25s
10.	CORNAGGIA-PREMOLI	ALFA ROMEO	17h 48m 50s

6TH MILLE MIGLIA : 9–10 APRIL 1932.
STARTERS 88. FINISHERS 42.

1.	BORZACCHINI-BIGNAMI	ALFA ROMEO 68.67 mph	14h 55m 19s
2.	TROSSI-BRIVIO	ALFA ROMEO	15h 10m 59s
3.	SCARFIOTTI-D'IPPOLITO	ALFA ROMEO	15h 44m 41s
4.	MINOIA-BALESTRIERI	ALFA ROMEO	16h 54m 37s
5.	CARRAROLI-GHERSI M.	ALFA ROMEO	17h 04m 03s
6.	GIULAY-VENTURI	ALFA ROMEO	17h 09m 14s
7.	SANTINELLI-BERTI	ALFA ROMEO	17h 10m 55s
8.	STRAZZA-GISMONDI	LANCIA	17h 14m 22s
9.	LURANI-CANAVESI	ALFA ROMEO	17h 22m 54s
10.	GAZZABINI-DIAZ	ALFA ROMEO	17h 26m 21s

7TH MILLE MIGLIA : 8–9 APRIL 1933.
STARTERS 85. FINISHERS 52.

1.	NUVOLARI-COMPAGNONI	ALFA ROMEO 67.85 mph	15h 11m 50s
2.	CASTELBARCO-CORTESE	ALFA ROMEO	15h 38m 02s
3.	TARUFFI-PELLEGRINI	ALFA ROMEO	16h 00m 57s
4.	BATTAGLIA-BIANCHI	ALFA ROMEO	16h 19m 40s
5.	SCARFIOTTI-D'IPPOLITO	ALFA ROMEO	16h 22m 10s
6.	SANTINELLI-BERTI	ALFA ROMEO	16h 25m 39s
7.	RUESCH-KESSLER	ALFA ROMEO	16h 25m 46s
8.	GAZZABINI-D'ALESSIO	ALFA ROMEO	16h 31m 28s
9.	FOLIGNO-COMOTTI	ALFA ROMEO	16h 41m 48s
10.	PEVERELLI-DELL'ORTO	ALFA ROMEO	16h 51m 55s

8TH MILLE MIGLIA : 8–9 APRIL 1934.
STARTERS 57. FINISHERS 29.

1.	VARZI-BIGNAMI	ALFA ROMEO 71.44 mph	14h 08m 05s
2.	NUVOLARI-SIENA	ALFA ROMEO	14h 16m 58s
3.	CHIRON-ROSA	ALFA ROMEO	15h 24m 00s
4.	BATTAGLIA-BIANCHI	ALFA ROMEO	15h 29m 35s
5.	TARUFFI-BERTOCCHI	MASERATI	15h 39m 01s
6.	SANGUINETTI-BALESTRERO	ALFA ROMEO	16h 21m 31s
7.	DUSIO-AJMINI	ALFA ROMEO	16h 38m 10s
8.	AURICCHIO-BERTI	ALFA ROMEO	16h 43m 17s
9.	PERTILE-JONOCH	ALFA ROMEO	16h 55m 29s
10.	NARDILLI-PINTACUDA	LANCIA	16h 58m 56s

**9TH MILLE MIGLIA : 14–15 APRIL 1935.
STARTERS 86. FINISHERS 47.**

1.	PINTACUDA-DELLA STUFA	ALFA ROMEO 71.72 mph	14h 04m 47s
2.	TADINI-CHIARI	ALFA ROMEO	14h 46m 38s
3.	BATTAGLIA-TUFFANELLI	ALFA ROMEO	15h 04m 08s
4.	RUESCH-GUATTA	ALFA ROMEO	15h 05m 59s
5.	MACCHIA-DANESE	ALFA ROMEO	15h 10m 58s
6.	SANGUINETTI-BALESTRERO	ALFA ROMEO	15h 12m 47s
7.	BIANCO-BERTOCCHI	MASERATI	15h 12m 56s
8.	CORTESE-SEVERI	ALFA ROMEO	15h 26m 45s
9.	GURGO SALICE-LAREDO	ALFA ROMEO	15h 39m 01s
10.	ROSA-COMOTTI	ALFA ROMEO	15h 56m 43s

**10th MILLE MIGLIA : 5–6 APRIL 1936.
STARTERS 69. FINISHERS 37.**

1.	BRIVIO-ONGARO	ALFA ROMEO 76.01 mph	13h 07m 51s
2.	FARINA-MEAZZA	ALFA ROMEO	13h 08m 23s
3.	PINTACUDA-STEFANI	ALFA ROMEO	13h 44m 17s
4.	BIONDETTI-CESARA	ALFA ROMEO	13h 59m 21s
5.	TENNI-BERTOCCHI	MASERATI	14h 18m 40s
6.	BIANCO-BOCCALI	MASERATI	14h 55m 10s
7.	DE RHAM-BANTI	ALFA ROMEO	15h 35m 35s
8.	GURGO SALICE-LAREDO	ALFA ROMEO	15h 45m 27s
9.	CATTANEO-DONATI	ALFA ROMEO	15h 59m 07s
10.	ROCCO-FILIPPONE	MASERATI	16h 14m 32s

**11TH MILLE MIGLIA : 4–5 APRIL 1937.
STARTERS 124. FINISHERS 65.**

1.	PINTACUDA-MAMBELLI	ALFA ROMEO 71.71 mph	14h 17m 32s
2.	FARINA-MEAZZA	ALFA ROMEO	14h 35m 11s
3.	SCHELL-CARRIÈRE	DELAHAYE	14h 54m 55s
4.	BORATTO-GUIDOTTI	ALFA ROMEO	15h 40m 01s
5.	'VENTIDUE'-'VENTUNO'	ALFA ROMEO	16h 19m 45s
6.	CORTESE-GUATTA	ALFA ROMEO	16h 21m 20s
7.	CRIVELLARI-FERRARO	ALFA ROMEO	17h 04m 25s
8.	TEAGNO-BARBIERI	ALFA ROMEO	17h 04m 33s
9.	SEVERI-RIGHETTI	ALFA ROMEO	17h 09m 20s
10.	CONTINI-SALVADORI	ALFA ROMEO	17h 09m 35s

**12TH MILLE MIGLIA : 3–4 APRIL 1938.
STARTERS 141. FINISHERS 72.**

1.	BIONDETTI-STEFANI	ALFA ROMEO 84.61 mph	11h 58m 29s
2.	PINTACUDA-MAMBELLI	ALFA ROMEO	12h 00m 31s
3.	DUSIO-BONINSEGNI	ALFA ROMEO	12h 37m 31s
4.	DREYFUS-VARET	DELAHAYE	12h 39m 53s
5.	CARRIÈRE-VANDERPYL	TALBOT	12h 59m 03s
6.	'VENTIDUE'-'VENTUNO'	ALFA ROMEO	13h 28m 53s
7.	MAZAUD-QUINLIN	DELAHAYE	13h 33m 41s
8.	FANE-JAMES	BMW	13h 36m 19s
9.	CORTESE-FUMAGALLI	ALFA ROMEO	13h 38m 11s
10.	LURANI-SCHAUMBURG	BMW	13h 38m 52s

Tragically the twelfth Mille Miglia was to be one of the most important in the whole series between 1927 and 1957. Weather conditions were perfect and the race was run at a record-breaking average speed. In Bologna a Lancia Aprilia, driven by

CONTE MAGGI'S MILLE MIGLIA

Bruzzo and Mignanego from Genoa, somersaulted into the crowd after crossing a tramline, killing ten people, including seven children, and causing the race to be banned in 1939.

Britain was already at war with Germany on 28 April 1940, but Italy had not at that time declared war on Great Britain, although it was to do so shortly. It was on that date that the thirteenth Mille Miglia, or to give the race its correct title, the `1st Gran Premio Brescia delle Mille Miglia' was held on a nine lap triangular Brescia–Cremona–Mantua–Brescia 103.1 mile circuit, or 927 miles.

13TH MILLE MIGLIA : 28 APRIL 1940.
STARTERS 88. FINISHERS 33.

1.	von HANSTEIN-BAUMER	BMW 104.20 mph	8h 54m 46s
2.	FARINA-MAMBELLI	ALFA ROMEO	9h 10m 16s
3.	BRUDES-ROESE	BMW	9h 13m 27s
4.	BIONDETTI-STEFANI	ALFA ROMEO	9h 13m 37s
5.	BRIEM-RICHTER	BMW	9h 16m 08s
6.	WENCHER-SCHOLTZ	BMW	9h 17m 15s
7.	PINTACUDA-SANESI	ALFA ROMEO	9h 25m 47s
8.	TROSSI-LUCCHI	ALFA ROMEO	9h 36m 55s
9.	FIORUZZI-SOLA	FIAT	11h 11m 47s
10.	BERTANI-LASAGNI	FIAT	11h 16m 46s

14TH MILLE MIGLIA : 21–22 JUNE 1947.
STARTERS 155. FINISHERS 54.

1.	ROMANO-BIONDETTI	ALFA ROMEO 70.14 mph	16h 16m 39s
2.	NUVOLARI-CARENA	CISITALIA	16h 32m 35s
3.	BERNABEI-PACINI	CISITALIA	16h 38m 17s
4.	MINETTI-FACETTI	CISITALIA	17h 00m 40s
5.	CAPELLI-GERLI	FIAT	17h 17m 38s

6.	DELLA CHIESA-BRANDOLI	FIAT	17h 26m 04s
7.	ERMINI-QUENTIN	FIAT	17h 27m 37s
8.	COMIRATO-COMIRATO	FIAT	17h 27m 45s
9.	BALESTRERO-BRACCO	FIAT	17h 31m 44s
10.	GURGO SALICE-CORNAGGIA	ALFA ROMEO	17h 51m 55s

15TH MILLE MIGLIA : 1–2 MAY 1948.
STARTERS 167. FINISHERS 64.

1.	BIONDETTI-NAVONE	FERRARI 75.76 mph	15h 05m 44s
2.	COMIRATO-DUMAS	FIAT	16h 33m 08s
3.	APRUZZI F.-APRUZZI A.	FIAT	16h 52m 30s
4.	TERIGI-BERTI	FIAT	16h 57m 10s
5.	SCAGLIARINI G.-MAFFIODO	CISITALIA	17h 00m 05s
6.	BIANCHETTI-CORNAGGIA	ALFA ROMEO	17h 02m 43s
7.	SCAGLIARINI C.-MASI	FIAT	17h 14m 39s
8.	CHRISTILLIN-NASI	FIAT	17h 17m 04s
9.	HEALEY D.-HEALEY G.	HEALEY	17h 26m 10s
10.	COLNAGHI-POZZONI	FIAT	17h 27m 56s

16TH MILLE MIGLIA : 24–25 APRIL 1949.
STARTERS 303. FINISHERS 182.

1.	BIONDETTI-SALANI	FERRARI 82.16 mph	12h 07m 05s
2.	BONETTO-CARP		12h 35m 07s
3.	ROL-RICHIERO	ALFA ROMEO	12h 51m 10s
4.	AURICCHIO-BOZZINI	FIAT	13h 57m 52s

CONTE MAGGI'S MILLE MIGLIA

5. SCAGLIARINI-MAGGIO	CISITALIA	14h 09m 42s
6. BASSI-BRAMBILLA	FIAT	14h 12m 43s
7. APRILE-BOSSETTI	MASERATI	14h 17m 51s
8. ADANTI-MALLUCCI	FIAT	14h 18m 59s
9. CAPELLI-VERONESI	FIAT	14h 21m 49s
10. HEALEY G.-WISDOM	HEALEY	14h 24m 03s

17TH MILLE MIGLIA : 23–24 APRIL 1950. STARTERS 375. FINISHERS 213.

1. MARZOTTO G.-CROSARA	FERRARI 77.00 mph	13h 39m 20s
2. SERAFINI-SALANI	FERRARI	13h 46m 53s
3. FANGIO-ZANARDI	ALFA ROMEO	14h 02m 05s
4. BRACCO-MAGLIOLI	FERRARI	14h 07m 23s
5. JOHNSON-LEA	JAGUAR	14h 29m 27s
6. CORTESE-TERAVAZZI	FRAZER NASH	14h 33m 59s
7. FAGIOLI-DIOTALLEVI	OSCA	14h 34m 44s
8. BIONDETTI-BRONZONI	JAGUAR	14h 38m 39s
9. MARZOTTO V.-FONTANA	FERRARI	14h 39m 02s
10. SCHWELM-COLONNA	ALFA ROMEO	14h 45m 51s

18TH MILLE MIGLIA : 28–29 APRIL 1951. STARTERS 325. FINISHERS 175.

1. VILLORESI-CASSANI	FERRARI 76.13 mph	12h 50m 18s
2. BRACCO-MAGLIOLI	LANCIA AURELIA	13h 10m 14s
3. SCOTTI-RUSPAGGIARI	FERRARI	13h 22m 04s
4. MARZOTTO P.-MARINI	FERRARI	13h 30m 48s
5. 'IPPOCAMPO'-MORI	LANCIA AURELIA	13h 47m 30s
6. BONETTO-CASNAGHI	ALFA ROMEO	13h 49m 35s
7. VALENZANO-MAGGIO	LANCIA AURELIA	13h 50m 00s

8. FAGIOLI-BORGHI	OSCA	13h 52m 35s
9. CORTESE-TAGNI	FRAZER NASH	14h 06m 28s
10. BORDONI-SERBELLONI	OSCA	14h 06m 49s

19TH MILLE MIGLIA : 4–5 MAY 1952. STARTERS 501. FINISHERS 275.

1. BRACCO-ROLFO	FERRARI 80.36 mph	12h 09m 45s
2. KLING-KLENK	MERCEDES	12h 14m 17s
3. FAGIOLI-BORGHI	AURELIA	12h 40m 05s
4. CARACCIOLA-KURRIE	MERCEDES	12h 48m 29s
5. ANSELMI-SEMINO	AURELIA	12h 54m 06s
6. 'IPPOCAMPO'-MORI	AURELIA	13h 05m 39s
7. JOHNSON-MACKENZIE	NASH-HEALEY	13h 11m 59s
8. AMENDOLA-PINZERO	AURELIA	13h 12m 18s
9. BRIVIO-CASSANI	FERRARI	13h 14m 22s
10. BORDONI-GERONIMO	FERRARI	13h 19m 58s

20TH MILLE MIGLIA : 25–26 APRIL 1953. STARTERS 481. FINISHERS 286.

1. MARZOTTO G.-CROSARA	FERRARI 88.96 mph	10h 37m 19s
2. FANGIO-SALA	ALFA ROMEO	10h 49m 03s
3. BONETTO-PERUZZI	LANCIA	11h 07m 40s
4. COLE-VANDELLI	FERRARI	11h 20m 39s
5. PARNELL-KLEMENTASKY	ASTON MARTIN	11h 32m 43s
6. GILETTI-BERTOCCHI	MASERATI	11h 38m 42s
7. MAGGIO-ANSELMI	LANCIA	11h 41m 07s
8. BIONDETTI-BAROVERO	LANCIA	11h 49m 49s
9. CABIANCA-ROGHI	FERRARI	11h 51m 39s
10. MANTOVANI-PALAZZI	MASERATI	11h 51m 56s

CONTE MAGGI'S MILLE MIGLIA

21ST MILLE MIGLIA : 1–2 MAY 1954.
STARTERS 374. FINISHERS 275.

1.	ASCARI, ALBERTO	LANCIA 87.27 mph	11h 26m 10s
2.	MARZOTTO V.	FERRARI	12h 00m 01s
3.	MUSSO L.-ZOCCO	MASERATI	12h 00m 10s
4.	BIONDETTI	FERRARI	12h 15m 36s
5.	VENEZIAN-ORLANDI	MASERATI	12h 27m 43s
6.	HERRMANN-LINGE	PORSCHE	12h 35m 44s
7.	SERAFINI-MANCINI	LANCIA AURELIA	12h 47m 12s
8.	CARINI-ARTESANI	ALFA ROMEO	12h 51m 52s
9.	LETO di PRIOLO C.-LETO di PRIOLO D.	FIAT-ZAGATO	12h 52m 38s
10.	CABIANCA	OSCA	12h 55m 08s

A significant change to the regulations was introduced for the 1954 Mille Miglia, which really altered the entire concept of the race. Since its inception in 1927 the event had been considered to be for near standard series production sports and touring cars, although this was frequently overlooked, and there had to be two persons per car – either a senior driver with a second driver to share the wheel, or one driver, who was at the wheel for the whole 1,000 miles, with a travelling mechanic or passenger beside him. This rule was dropped in 1954, and as a result several potential winners were driven in the 1954, 1955, 1956 and 1957 events by single drivers in cars capable of speeds of 200 mph or even more. The more 'gentlemanly' touring car race, which had of course been contested every inch of the way, with cars often only seconds apart at the finish, turned into a far more lethal poker-game played for high stakes at very high speeds.

22ND MILLE MIGLIA : 1–2 MAY 1955.
STARTERS 521. FINISHERS 281.

1.	MOSS-JENKINSON	MERCEDES 98.53 mph	10h 07m 48s
2.	FANGIO	MERCEDES	10h 39m 33s
3.	MAGLIOLI	FERRARI	10h 52m 47s
4.	GIARDINI	MASERATI	11h 15m 32s
5.	FITCH	MERCEDES	11h 29m 31s
6.	SIGHINOLFI	FERRARI	11h 33m 27s
7.	GENDEBIEN	MERCEDES	11h 36m 00s
8.	SEIDEL	PORSCHE	12h 08m 17s
9.	BELLUCCI	MASERATI	12h 09m 10s
10.	CASELLA	MERCEDES	12h 11m 15s

23RD MILLE MIGLIA : 29–30 APRIL 1956.
STARTERS 365. FINISHERS 182.

1.	CASTELLOTTI	FERRARI 85.90 mph	11h 37m 10s
2.	COLLINS-KLEMENTASKY	FERRARI	11h 49m 28s
3.	MUSSO	FERRARI	12h 11m 49s
4.	FANGIO	FERRARI	12h 26m 50s
5.	GENDEBIEN-WASHER	FERRARI	12h 29m 58s
6.	METTERNICH-EINSIEDEL	MERCEDES	12h 36m 38s
7.	SEIDEL-GLOCKLER	MERCEDES	12h 38m 24s
8.	POLLET-FLAMDRAX	MERCEDES	12h 49m 56s
9.	CABIANCA	OSCA	12h 57m 11s
10.	RIESS-HERMANN	MERCEDES	13h 06m 31s

24TH MILLE MIGLIA : 12–13 MAY 1957.
STARTERS 298. FINISHERS 163.

1.	TARUFFI	FERRARI 95.39 mph	10h 27m 47s
2.	VON TRIPS	FERRARI	10h 30m 48s
3.	GENDEBIEN-WASHER	FERRARI	10h 35m 52s
4.	SCARLATTI	MASERATI	11h 00m 58s
5.	MAGLIOLI	PORSCHE	11h 14m 07s

6. LUGLIO-CARLI	FERRARI	11h 26m 58s	
7. 'IPPOCRATE'	FERRARI	11h 30m 55s	
8. MUNARON G.	FERRARI	11h 32m 04s	
9. BUTICCHI	FERRARI	11h 44m 27s	
10. KOECHERT	FERRARI	11h 49m 02s	

1ST–10TH PLACE POSITION LEAGUE TABLE BY MAKE

ALFA ROMEO	97 (Winner 1928, 1929, 1930, 1932, 1933, 1934, 1935, 1936, 1937, 1938 and 1947)
FERRARI	32 (Winner 1948, 1949, 1950, 1951, 1952, 1953, 1956 and 1957)
LANCIA	20 (Winner 1954)
FIAT	18
MASERATI	15
MERCEDES	13 (Winner 1931 and 1955)
OM	10 (Winner 1927)
BMW	6 (Winner 1940)
CISITALIA	5
OSCA	5
DELAHAYE	3
PORSCHE	3
FRAZER NASH	2
HEALEY	2
JAGUAR	2
ASTON MARTIN	1
BIANCHI	1
BUGATTI	1
ISOTTA FRASCHINI	1
ITALA	1
NASH-HEALEY	1
TALBOT	1

WINNER LEAGUE TABLE BY MAKE

ALFA ROMEO	11 (from 1928)
FERRARI	8 (from 1948)
MERCEDES	2 (from 1931)
OM	1 (from 1927)
BMW	1 (from 1940)
LANCIA	1 (from 1954)

APPENDIX 3
The '1000 MIGLIA'

The '1000 Miglia' club, which still meets regularly in Brescia, kept full documentation of all drivers and passengers in the Mille Miglia. Membership rules were quite simple: in any year the applicant had to have completed the full 1,000 miles. So, for example, one sees that Piero Taruffi, who won the race in his Ferrari in 1957 at his fifteenth attempt, is shown as having completed only five Mille Miglia in 1930, 1933, 1934, 1938 and in 1957, his victory year, and that the veteran driver from Colombaro, Brescia, Giacomo Ragnoli, who competed fourteen times, finished on eight of those, putting him on equal terms with the legendary Tazio Nuvolari. Some drivers retired within a few hundred metres of leaving the starting ramp; others failed with the chequered flag in sight.

The '1000 MIGLIA' lists every finisher, but here we salute those who finished the gruelling course between six and fourteen times:

14 CORTESE, from 1927

13 CORNAGGIA, from 1931

12 ROSA, from 1927

11 FACCHETTI, from 1927

9 APRUZZI F., from 1931
BIONDETTI, from 1936
CAPELLI, from 1937
LURANI, from 1932

8 NUVOLARI, from 1927
RAGNOLI, from 1935
CABIANCA, from 1949

7 PINTACUDA, from 1929
MORELLI, from 1949

6 ANSELMI, from 1948
BALESTRERO, from 1927
BERLUCCHI, from 1949
BERTI, from 1932
BERTOCCHI, from 1931
BOLOGNESI, from 1929
CRIVELLARI, from 1948
CONCARI, from 1927
GAZZABINI, from 1928
'FRATE IGNOTO', from 1927 (pseudonym of MERCANTI, Arturo)
SCARFIOTTI, from 1928
CODA, from 1931
GUIDOTTI, from 1931
ROMANO, from 1927
CAPELLO, from 1927
DE SANCTIS, from 1938
GUARNIERI, from 1950
SALICE, from 1935
MERLI, from 1950
MANDRINI, from 1938
OGNA, from 1938
STANGA, from 1949
VENEZIAN, from 1949

Appendix 4:
Route Maps of the Mille Miglia

The Mille Miglia story started in 1927, when the motor car was still a comparatively rare sight on Italian roads, and ended three decades later in 1957. By sad coincidence, World War II acted as a buffer in the Mille Miglia calendar. There were eleven pre-war races for super charged cars up to 1939; one staged on a closed circuit around Brescia in 1940, when much of Europe was already under German occupation, and another twelve post-war races with super-chargers banned, but speeds increased dramatically.

Two further developments played a major part in entirely altering the concept of the race and paradoxically brought about its downfall. In August 1953 the great Italian ace Tazio Nuvolari died after a long and painful lung infection caused by the inhalation of toxic exhaust fumes over many years of racing. The Italian nation mourned the death of its worthy champion and in his honour the Mille Miglia race organisers created a special prize for the 1954 race. This was known as the Tazio Nuvolari trophy, or 'il Gran Premio Tazio Nuvolari' and was awarded for the fastest time recorded on the final section of the race, Cremona–Mantua (Nuvolari's home town) –Brescia, over 82 miles of ultra-fast road and much of it along the autostrada.

In order to justify the introduction of this high-speed section – which was not without its severe critics – the race officials relaxed another rule which had been enforced for more than a quarter of a century, whereby a second driver had to be in the car throughout the race. From 1954 onwards drivers were allowed to be single-handed.

Suddenly the race was transformed. The Mille Miglia had been conceived as a 1,000 mile race over open roads for touring cars, which were originally as near standard as possible, and in which the car and its crew would be tested to the limit in exhausting road and weather conditions. In 1954, with the amended rule in operation, it was turned into a flat-out race for sports and grand touring cars with lone drivers motoring at speeds up to 200 mph or more, and overall race times tumbled. The factories decided that there could be more publicity for 'attacking' driving by popular individualists, and so in the next four years, until the race was banned in

1957, millions of race fans saw superb solo performances turned in by Alberto Ascari, Vittorio Marzotto, Juan Manuel-Fangio, Umberto Maglioli, Castellotti, Luigi Musso, Piero Taruffi and Wolfgang von Trips.

Three of the last four races held were won by drivers with no passenger: Ascari, 1954 (Lancia), Castellotti 1956 (Ferrari) and Taruffi 1957 (Ferrari); in 1957 the first three cars covered the 1,000 miles in under eleven hours, only two of the top ten overall had a co-driver and *all* of those ten completed the distances in under twelve hours – an average of around 85 mph.

The name of the Mille Miglia signified a 1,000 mile race, but not every race had the same exact overall distance. There were wide variations, from the 928 miles in 1940 when it was held as a 9-lap circuit race around Brescia, to the 1,139 miles of the 1947 and 1948 events, the extra distance being because of the slow post-war road rebuilding, after most of the bridges across the river Po had been destroyed in 1945.

There were twelve changes of route for the Mille Miglia in the twenty-four editions. In theory the race was run on a closed circuit with roads free from traffic, but on a route of such length this was impossible to guarantee, particularly from 1950 onwards as the number of competing cars reached alarming proportions. In 1953, for example, 575 cars started at thirty second or one minute intervals from late on the Saturday evening until after seven on the Sunday morning, spread over at least nine hours. When Stirling Moss won in 1955, his start time with the Mercedes was 7.22 a.m. and he was back in Brescia again 10 hours 7 minutes later, while other cars which had left over ten hours before him did not return for another four hours.

With this wide diversification in overall speed and elapsed time over the 1,000 mile route it was almost certain that near-misses or accidents involving civilian transport would happen. One of the worst occurred in 1937, when the 2-litre MG Magnette of British journalist Tommy Wisdom and his wife Billy, both of whom were well known at Brooklands in pre-war races, was hit head-on by a private car outside Florence. There were also frequent avoidances of cyclists and sadly

CONTE MAGGI'S MILLE MIGLIA

several collisions resulting in injury or death, and the full extent of the damage to property or the number of race fans who were actually maimed or injured by competing cars has probably never been compiled.

Soon after each year's race conte Aymo Maggi and Renzo Castagneto undertook a frank and thorough investigation of the race, using constructive criticism in order to amend or improve the following year's event. This sometimes involved major route changes, for physical or political reasons, and sometimes quite minor ones, where a small section would be re-routed because it may have caused problems with the police, or the Italian army, who did a magnificent job over the years in controlling the circuit. There were many manned and unmanned level-crossings to be noted and the timetables of express trains were frequently re-scheduled to ensure that cars in the fastest sports car classes had a clear run on the Sunday morning.

Before describing the twelve different routes used, it should be noted that in some years, cars left Brescia and completed the 1,000 mile circuit in an anti-clockwise direction and in other years in a clockwise direction, when the Adriatic coastal section was covered from north to south. The race was always run in late April or early May and a driver could expect mixed weather conditions with some sun, frequent heavy rain storms and fog with visibility down to 30 yards at times. On each section the driver had to make two or three stops for fuel and tyres and would have to pass through at least eight *controlli*, or controls, where a route-card would be quickly stamped — frequently while the car was still moving slowly — by an Automobile Club official. This was to ensure no short cuts were taken.

An equivalent British 1,000 mile race, starting and finishing in Thirsk, Yorkshire, can be seen plotted right. The race would run in a clockwise direction, via York, King's Lynn, London, Brighton, Southampton, Exeter, Bath, Oxford, Leicester, Manchester, Lancaster and Kendal. If Stirling Moss's 1955 record 10 hour 7 minute race had been run on this circuit, he would have had to leave Thirsk at 7.22 a.m. and have arrived back at 5.29 p.m. the same day, thus achieving an average overall speed of 98.53 mph.

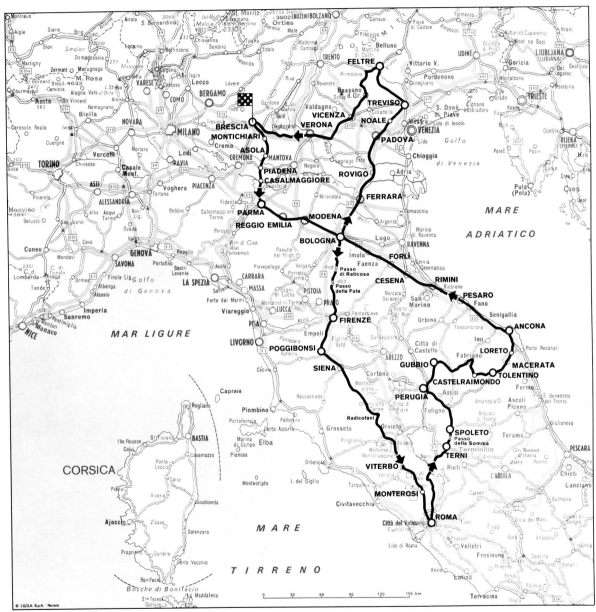

1927–
1928–
1929–
1930–

Left Brescia in a south-
westerly direction, anti-
clockwise, ASOLA,
PARMA, BOLOGNA
(first time), RATICOSA
AND FUTA PASSES,
FLORENCE, SIENA,
ROME, TERNI, GUBBIO,
LORETO, ANCONA,
PESARO, FORLI,
BOLOGNA (second
passage), FERRARA,
PADOVA, TREVISO,
FELTRE, VICENZA,
VERONA, BRESCIA. At
least one-third was on
dirt roads, and there
were 67 level-
crossings, many
unmanned. 1,628
kilometres, 1,017 miles.

CONTE MAGGI'S MILLE MIGLIA

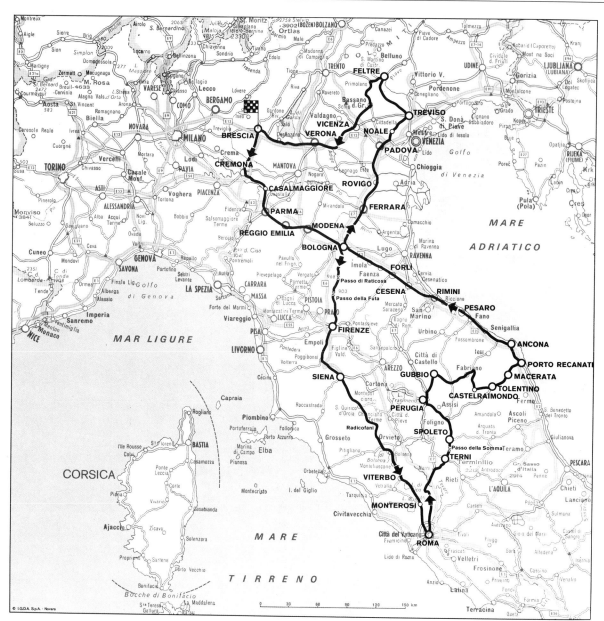

Left Brescia in a south-westerly direction, anti-clockwise, CREMONA, MODENA, BOLOGNA (first time), FLORENCE, SIENA, ROME, TERNI, GUBBIO, ANCONA, BOLOGNA (second passage), PADOVA, TREVISO, FELTRE, VICENZA, VERONA, BRESCIA. It included many roads with dirt surfaces and was bumpy, causing frequent punctures. 1,635 kilometres, 1,021 miles.

1934–
1935–
1937

Left Brescia in a south-westerly direction, anti-clockwise, PIACENZA, MODENA, BOLOGNA (first time), SIENA, ROME, GUBBIO, ANCONA, RIMINI, BOLOGNA (second passage), PADOVA, VENICE, TREVISO, VICENZA, BRESCIA. Road conditions improved, with a high-speed run across a lagoon bridge to Venice. The tough alpine section to Feltre was removed. 1,615 kilometres, 1,009 miles.

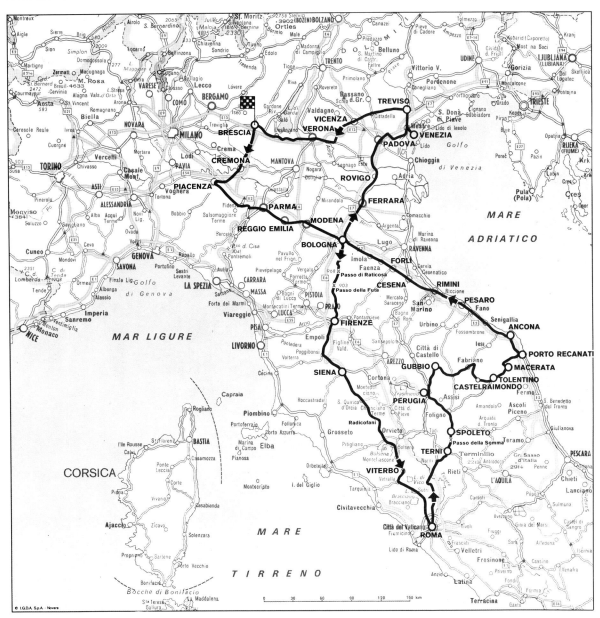

CONTE MAGGI'S MILLE MIGLIA

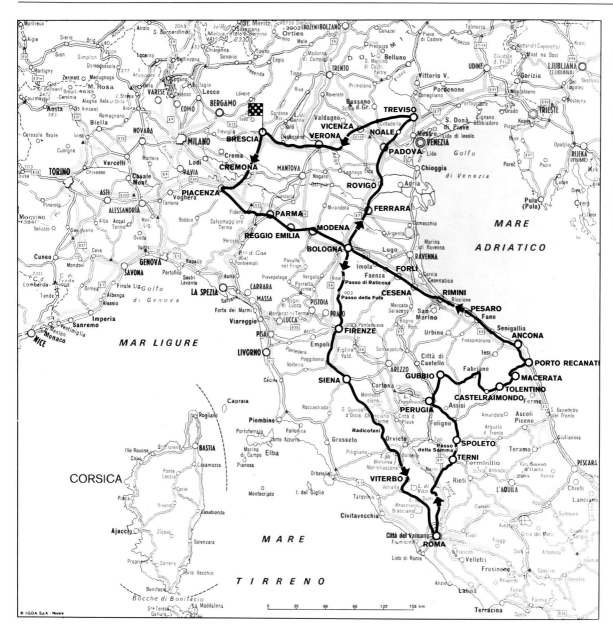

1936

Left Brescia in a south-westerly direction, anti-clockwise, PIACENZA, MODENA, BOLOGNA (first time), SIENA, ROME, GUBBIO, ANCONA, BOLOGNA (second passage) PADOVA, TREVISO, VERONA, BRESCIA. The run to Venice was removed, there was no alpine section, and it was less arduous. This tenth edition was the shortest of the pre-war races. 1,597 kilometres, 998 miles.

CONTE MAGGI'S MILLE MIGLIA

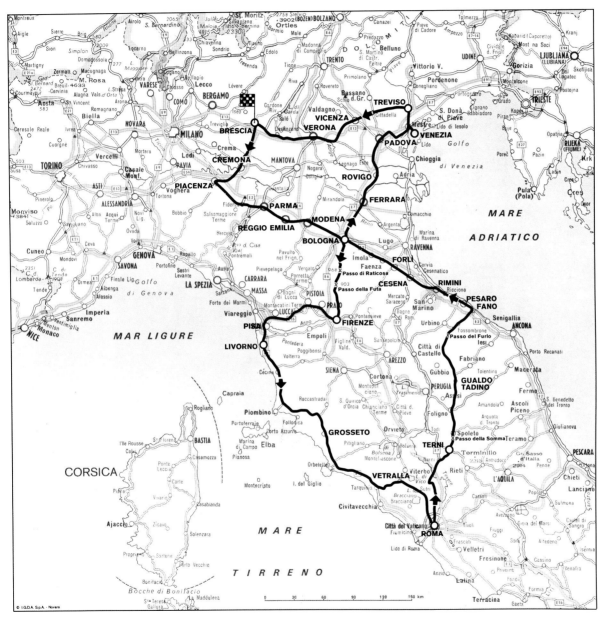

1938

Left Brescia in a south-westerly direction, anti-clockwise, PIACENZA, MODENA, BOLOGNA (first time), FLORENCE, PISA, LIVORNO, GROSSETO, ROME, TERNI, FANO, BOLOGNA (second passage), VENICE, VERONA, BRESCIA. A substantial route change brought in a long run down the west coast, cut out the mountainous sections after Rome, included Venice again and removed the alpine section. It was designed to ensure a much faster race and Clemente Biondetti won in under twelve hours. 1,621 kilometres, 1,013 miles.

CONTE MAGGI'S MILLE MIGLIA

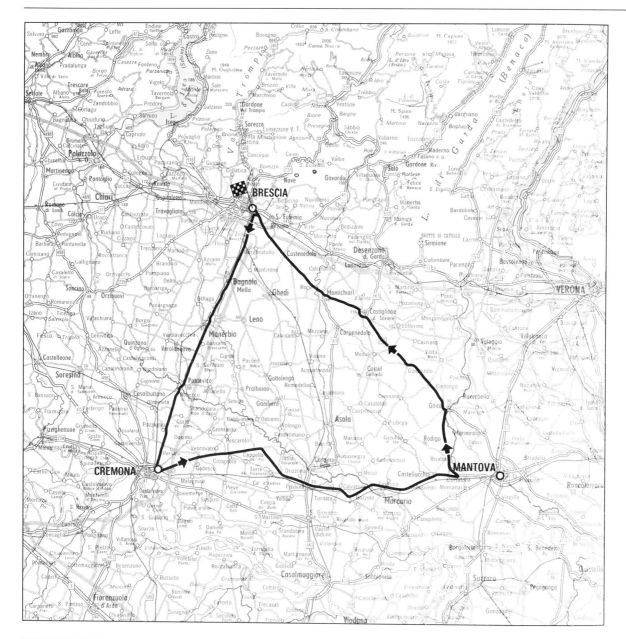

1940

The BRESCIA-
CREMONA-BRESCIA
circuit race, run in an
anti-clockwise
direction on the old
Settimana di Brescia
circuit of the early
1900s, after the 1939
race had been
banned. It made a
very fast, triangular
circuit, nine laps of
103 miles. This
thirteenth edition was
officially the '1st Gran
Premio Brescia della
Mille Miglia' and not
the Mille Miglia, but
everyone considers it
the thirteenth race.
1,485 kilometres, 927
miles.

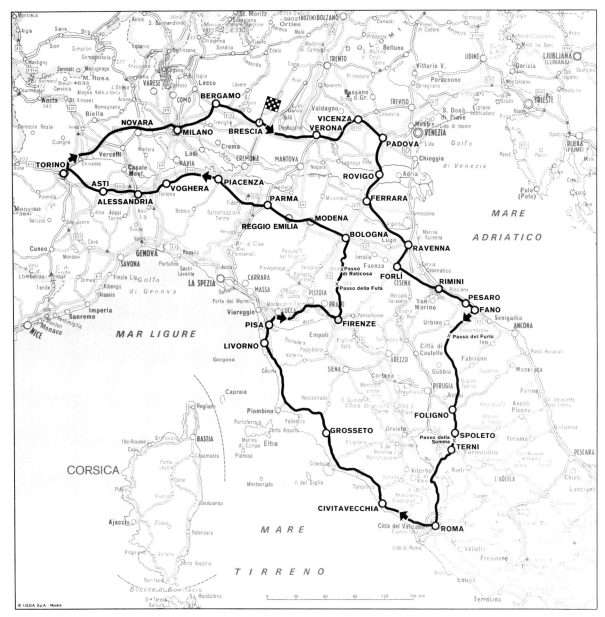

1947–1948

Left Brescia due east, for the first time in a clockwise direction, PADOVA, RAVENNA, FANO, TERNI, ROME, GROSSETO, LIVORNO, FLORENCE, BOLOGNA, PIACENZA, TURIN, NOVARA, MILAN, BERGAMO, BRESCIA. Only the persistence of conte Aymo Maggi put the Mille Miglia back on the map, despite acute problems with damaged roads, broken bridges and shattered communications. Bologna could not handle a double passage and a long, tedious autostrada section via Turin and Milan was included to make up the distance, as many of the Po valley bridges were impassable. 1,823 kilometres, 1,139 miles.

CONTE MAGGI'S MILLE MIGLIA

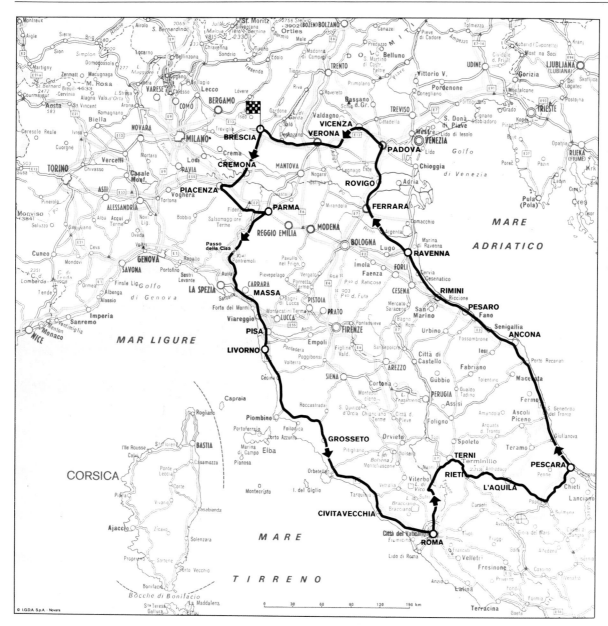

1949

Left Brescia, in a south-westerly direction, anti-clockwise again, PARMA, LIVORNO, ROME, TERNI, L'AQUILA PESCARA, RAVENNA, PADOVA, VERONA, BRESCIA. Considerable changes, again to ensure fast times, but the introduction of the Rome-L'Aquila-Pescara section meant a tricky double-crossing of the Apennines before a long sprint along the Adriatic coast. Bologna was eliminated, but was back again the following year. 1,593 kilometres, 995 miles.

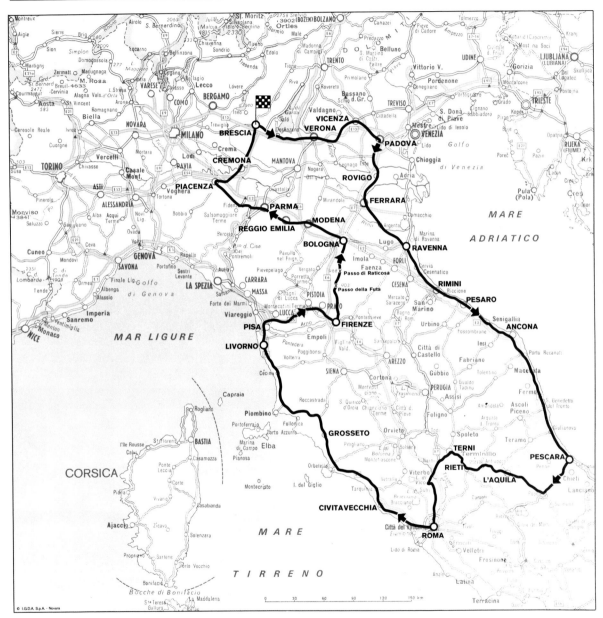

1950

Left Brescia, due east to PADOVA, all the way down the Adriatic coast to PESCARA, TERNI, ROME, GROSSETO, LIVORNO, PISA, FLORENCE, BOLOGNA, PIACENZA, BRESCIA. The route was clockwise and remained so until the race's end and was very fast as autostrada sections allowed top speeds. Pescara was still the south-east pivot of the route and this time cars headed south-west before the Apennines section to Rome. 1,635 kilometres, 1,021 miles.

CONTE MAGGI'S MILLE MIGLIA

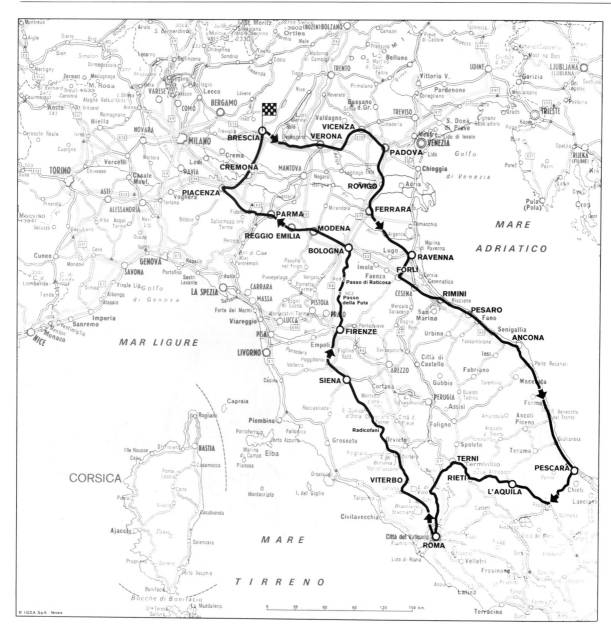

1951–

1952–

Left Brescia due east, clockwise direction, to VERONA, PADOVA, FORLI, ANCONA, PESCARA, ROME, SIENA, FLORENCE, BOLOGNA, PIACENZA, BRESCIA. After the changes of recent years, the route took on a more stable look, and fell into three obvious sections: Brescia-Pescara, Pescara-Siena and Siena-Brescia. The organisers did little to keep down speeds. 1,564 kilometres, 977 miles.

CONTE MAGGI'S MILLE MIGLIA

Left Brescia due east, clockwise direction, PADOVA, RIMINI, PESCARA, L'AQUILA, ROME, VITERBO, FLORENCE, BOLOGNA, PIACENZA, BRESCIA. There was a significant route change whereby Terni was cut out, making the passage to Rome shorter and easier. The organisers still encouraged faster speeds, many powerful sports cars competing for top honours. 1,512 kilometres, 945 miles.

CONTE MAGGI'S MILLE MIGLIA

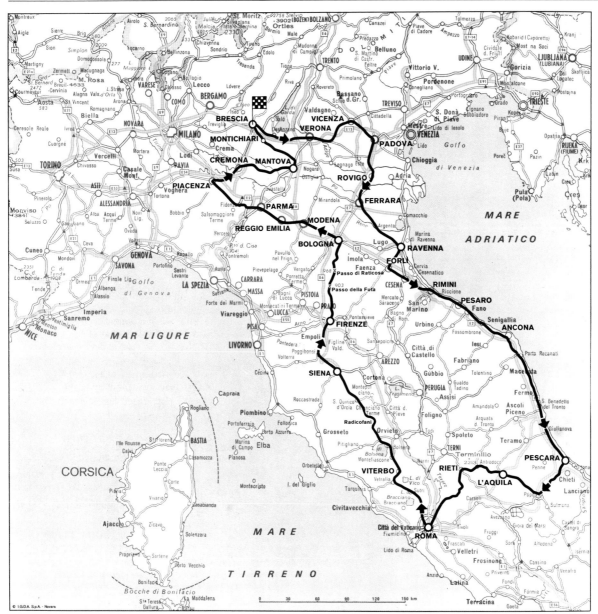

Following the death of Tazio Nuvolari in August 1953 the race organisers instituted a special 'Gran Premio Tazio Nuvolari' to include his birthplace at Mantua. Left Brescia, clockwise, due east to PADOVA, RIMINI, PESCARA, ROME, SIENA, BOLOGNA, MODENA, PIACENZA – then CREMONA–MANTUA–BRESCIA, specially-timed for the Nuvolari prize. There were 481 starters in 1953 and 521 in 1955 but the number reduced in 1956 to 365 cars. Due to the new section, the route was now very fast, critics saying dangerously so. The race was banned in 1957 following the death of Alfonso de Portago, co-driver Ed Nelson and ten spectators at Guidizzolo near the finish at Brescia. 1,597 kilometres, 998 miles.

INDEX

References to pictures are in Italic.

CONTE MAGGI'S MILLE MIGLIA